CONFESSIONS
OF AN
ENTREPRENEUR

'A hard hitting, no holds barred, crash course into
the world of the entrepreneur.'
Lord Bilimoria CBE DL, founder and chairman of Cobra Beer

'More like an outright thriller than a business book. It brings to life
the raw excitement and sheer terror of being an entrepreneur.'
Guy Browning, writer, broadcaster, creativity guru

'This is a fascinating account of what makes entrepreneurs tick; Chris
Robson has managed to map the DNA of successful entrepreneurs in
an entertaining and hugely readable way. It is a must read for anyone
wanting a window into the mind of the entrepreneur.'
Ronald Rudd, founder of Finsbury Communications

'If you are thinking of starting a business, this book makes
both interesting and entertaining reading.'
James Caan, CEO of Hamilton Bradshaw and star of *Dragons' Den*

'A truly remarkable book that will inspire, excite and occasionally
console any would-be entrepreneurs with creativity burning in their
soul. Chris Robson unlocks the human stories behind individuals
determined to shape the world and passes on tips about the lessons
learned from both success and failure.'
Greg Hadfield, award-winning journalist and internet entrepreneur

CONFESSIONS
OF AN
ENTREPRENEUR

How to survive
the highs and lows
of starting up

CHRIS ROBSON

Prentice Hall
Business
is an imprint of

Harlow, England • London • New York • Boston • San Francisco • Toronto • Sydney • Singapore • Hong Kong
Tokyo • Seoul • Taipei • New Delhi • Cape Town • Madrid • Mexico City • Amsterdam • Munich • Paris • Milan

PEARSON EDUCATION LIMITED

Edinburgh Gate
Harlow CM20 2JE
Tel: +44 (0)1279 623623
Fax: +44 (0)1279 431059
Website: www.pearsoned.co.uk

First published in Great Britain in 2010

Pearson Education is not responsible for the content of third party internet sites.

ISBN: 978-0-273-72148-2

British Library Cataloguing-in-Publication Data
A catalogue record for this book is available from the British Library

Library of Congress Cataloging-in-Publication Data
A catalog record for this book is available from the Library of Congress

10 9 8 7 6 5 4 3 2 1
14 13 12 11 10

Typeset in 11pt Minion Pro by 3
Printed and bound in Great Britain by Henry Ling Ltd, Dorchester, Dorset

This book is dedicated to my wife, Jo,
for giving me enormous strength, advice and love
and for enduring my obsession with my business

Introduction

WHAT IT'S ABOUT

This is not a textbook about writing a business plan or choosing the right business idea. Those books exist already. This doesn't.

This is a book about the emotional issues that other business books ignore – the sacrifices you make, the struggle to choose and work with the *right* partner(s), the strain of uncertainty and potential failure, the dizzying and addictive highs of success, the challenge of building and motivating a team – everything that you will experience when you start a new business. It's about the journey *every* entrepreneur has to take – and it's this journey, not just the destination, that you have to learn to love if you're going to be a great entrepreneur.

WHY I WROTE THIS BOOK

I wanted to bring this journey, warts and all, to life. To help you understand and feel what it's like to be an entrepreneur. I wanted to tell it as it is, no frills, so I've written this book 'live', whilst battling through my own start-up journey. I also wanted to make it broader, not just my story, so I spent time with other entrepreneurs, gaining their raw, invaluable insights. Inside you'll find out what it really takes, what you actually have to go through when you start a business. It is the emotional journey no-one ever told me about – maybe if they had, my life would have been very different!

I wish I had understood more about the emotional impact of starting a business when I started out, namely the toll it takes and the sheer amount of time it consumes. I think this toll is a rite of passage for any twenty-first-century business person. A company can be seen anywhere and anyone can copy any idea – it is 24/7 madness and all that this brings. This book isn't about how to avoid the madness, that's impossible, but it will help you to navigate through it.

HOW IT'S STRUCTURED AND WHY

Starting up can be less than a year for some people and more than five years for others, but the process involved is similar no matter how long it takes. The book is organised into four parts to mirror this process. The first part focuses on the excitement and preparation you feel before you start. The second part explores the inevitable strain that starts to surface as things get going. The third part goes further into the strain – when the going starts to get really tough and you may have to live without knowing which way is up. And, finally, the fourth part is when a sense of clarity emerges and you know whether the business will live or die and in what form – how do you deal with this and where do you go next?

Each chapter is based on a different emotional area, in the order in which you'll experience them as an entrepreneur.

WHAT DO I MEAN BY START-UP?

In my experience there are three types of 'new business' and each one leads to a different start-up journey.

Firstly, there is the entrepreneurial start-up. Although there are many different definitions, I define an entrepreneur as a person who starts a new enterprise, venture or idea and assumes significant accountability for the inherent risks and outcome. In other words, this is someone who has a new idea – something genuinely different, something innovative. This is Google or Innocent.

Secondly, there is a start-up of an existing and established business model. This could be starting a law firm, advertising agency or building company. Here the idea is rarely new or different, although it may be better, but the risks may still be great.

Thirdly, there are management buy-outs and buy-ins. This involves personal risk, mostly financial, but the big advantage is that the business is normally well established in an established business market.

I deal primarily with the first, but I shall talk about people in the second. Generally entrepreneurial ideas have less market proof, more risk and more stress. But all three business types have emotional issues. This is not a judgement about which is best. They all have a place and all can be just as rewarding, but often the people who embark on the entrepreneurial start-up have the least experience and knowledge. They're trying something new. It's a point in time, but is it the right time? Have they got the right idea? Is the business model clear? Have they done it before? Often the answer to each is no!

A LITTLE BIT ABOUT MY BACKGROUND

I started a new business, You Wish, at the beginning of this book with a profound belief that I had all the angles covered. I was feverishly excited about getting going. I couldn't wait to leave my highly paid job. I was going to conquer the world. I had a mould-breaking idea. After all, I had twenty years of business experience. I had been the youngest board director of ad agency DMB&B. I had built up and floated syzygy AG, a pan-European digital agency, for €240m in 2000 on the German Stock Exchange, at the end of the dotcom boom. I was a founder of Ink, now the world's largest producer of in-flight media. I had turned around Edengene, a strategy and innovation consultancy. And, across the years, advised and delivered solutions to a huge number of the world's biggest brands from Disney to Coca-Cola, Barclays to Santander and Citroen to Daimler Chrysler. I had also learnt from my own setbacks. I had plenty of business war stories and had never cracked – not yet ...

However, my journey, like most entrepreneurs, hasn't been a straight one and the business I've ended up with is not what I started out to do. But that's the thing about being an entrepreneur, you never quite know what the end result will be. And each time you start a new venture, you have to go all the way back to the beginning, start from scratch all over again.

Being an entrepreneur is a scary leveller in life. I was born into a privileged environment and went to Eton and Oxford. I could have taken an easier route, but, for some warped reason, I am drawn, time and time again, to all the pain of starting up. While I write this, for example, I am wondering if my latest business will sink or swim. Can I kick it into third gear, let alone fifth? Will my life be any better for doing this? Right now it's certainly a different one!

THE CONFESSIONS

Interviewing and hearing the confessions of the entrepreneurs featured in this book has been incredibly illuminating. It brings the issues to life and there are so many patterns and parallels amongst entrepreneurs to be drawn. I thought the highs and lows of my journey were fairly shocking, but I've gasped at what other entrepreneurs have been through.

I am fortunate that so many entrepreneurs have taken the time to talk so freely and honestly for the benefit of others. I have interviewed over twenty men and women in detail, all with different experiences and levels of success and failure. I have talked to all of them about their unique journey – their sacrifices, stresses, uncertainties and elation. They have all made honest, pertinent and invaluable comments for you to learn from. Although I reference various people in the book, I have only included people in the 'Entrepreneurs' section who I have actually interviewed in detail.

A FINAL NOTE BEFORE WE BEGIN

There are no guarantees of success when you start out on your journey – no matter how good you think you are and no matter how genius you think your idea is. The more you can prepare for the emotional roller coaster, the better. My story and the other confessions in here are designed to give you a snap shot of what's ahead – as they say, better the devil you know!

Best of luck in your quest and, most importantly, hang on to your humour!

About the entrepreneurs

I love the intensity, conviction and excitement of entrepreneurs. They are very different people. They challenge and want to be challenged. Life really is about dreams and ambitions. I wanted to try to capture some of this optimism, energy and honesty in this book. I wanted people who were smart and diverse in opinion and belief. I wanted people who would trust me and be prepared to be as open and honest as I was being. I wanted people who had really worked at it through thick and thin. I didn't want the typical business faces or heroes of business books and the myths and hype that surround them. I wanted it to be raw and revealing – small nuggets of insight, pleasure and pain.

I also wanted to capture, through my choice of entrepreneurs, the fact that men and women do often experience the entrepreneurial journey differently.

I have included entrepreneurs with businesses in fashion, temperature profiling, publishing, PR, retail, food manufacturing, TV production, payroll, music, market research, Internet, software, hospitality and plumbing. I admire all of these people and many of them are close friends. I am honoured to have seen inside their journeys. I hope that you feel the same.

VICTORIA BAILLIEU is a co-founder of Pay Check – a fully managed payroll business to the private sector and previously

Moneypenny Management. Victoria has a no-nonsense commitment and attitude to her business which her clients love.

JOHN BATES is Adjunct Professor of Entrepreneurship at London Business School, a director of Sussex Place Ventures and an entrepreneur, as founder, chairman and managing director of Datapaq, which has become the world's leading company for temperature profiling in hostile thermal environments. John inspired me at London Business School and has the drive and persistence of an entrepreneur and the clarity of a great teacher.

JANE BROWN was trained at Cordwainers College and is the founder of Jane Brown Shoes, who design, manufacture and sell luxury ladies' shoes. Jane is passionate and brilliant about shoes, but remarkably candid about the difficulties of running a fashion business, manufacturing and selling across the world.

PETER CHRISTIANSEN is a business school colleague and friend, with a razor-sharp mind and yet great kindness. He is the former Endemol UK MD, and founder of Zeal Television (a TV production company), Speedshape (a producer of high-end computer graphics for automotive advertising) and Precious Media (a content marketing agency).

MARK DE WESSELOW is co-founder of Square Meal, a publisher of on- and offline restaurant, event and drink sector information. He is an old friend and saw this opportunity long before the Internet arrived and has shown real commitment with his business partner, Simon White, in making it successful.

HUGO DIXON is an awesomely smart economist and *Financial Times* journalist, and formerly head of Lex. He was Business Journalist of the Year 2000 in the British Press Awards. He is co-founder of Breakingviews, a media company providing agenda-setting financial insight founded in 2000 and sold to Thomson Reuters in 2009.

JO FAIRLEY is a former editor of *Look Now* and *Honey* magazines and the co-founder of Green & Black's, the world's first organic chocolate, which was later sold to Cadbury. Jo breaks all my rules and created a successful business with her husband, Craig Sams, which is cool.

GEOFFREY GESTETNER is an old friend and a boxing blue and shows real passion for basic industry, which is so rare today. Geoffrey and I both worked at Hanson, but he had rather more interest in plumbing than I did! He is CEO of Cistermiser and Davidson Holdings. Cistermiser design, manufacture and distribute washroom control products including urinal flush control valves and hands-free WC flush valves for the industrial, commercial and domestic environment.

BILL GROSS is a serial entrepreneur and an Internet hero. He is a brilliant thinker and innovator who started and sold two software companies before founding Idealab in 1996. He is chairman and CEO of Idealab, a technical incubator in California that creates, builds and operates new companies. It has formed and operated 75 companies with 30 IPOs and acquisitions.

GREG HADFIELD is a former client of mine at syzygy. He is a friend and fellow Internet enthusiast. He is a *Sunday Times* journalist by background and co-founder of Soccernet (an online football newspaper launched in 1995 and sold to ESPN in 1999) and Schoolsnet (an online schools directory and portal launched in 1999 and sold to Hotcourses).

TOM HADFIELD is Greg's son and the co-founder of Soccernet and Schoolsnet. At syzygy we were all rather impressed by his quiet brilliance when he was still at school!

SEBASTIAN JAMES is an entrepreneur and co-founder of Silverscreen, a DVD retailer, and also a co-founder of eSubstance, which became Ink Publishing. He is now a director of Dixons (DSGI) and is smart, analytical and entertaining.

CLAIRE MASON is a brilliant business woman and PR. She is the founder of Man Bites Dog, a PR consultancy which won New Consultancy of the Year in the UK PR Week Awards in 2007. She is dripping with enthusiasm, like her amusing company name, and has spectacular focus.

SUE VAN MEETEREN is the former deputy chairman of Research International and co-founder of Jigsaw Research, a very successful medium-sized research consultancy to large organisations.

INGRID MURRAY is razor sharp and a quietly confident serial entrepreneur. She is co-founder of Inspop/Confused.com (a car insurance price comparison site that was sold to Admiral Insurance) and Ninah Consulting (a management consultancy for marketers that was sold to ZenithOptimedia) and founder of WeBuyNearby (a new online supermarket providing local fresh food).

MATT NORTON is a former syzygy colleague. He is smart and committed and has shown unbelievable resilience and entrepreneurial aptitude as the co-founder of Sentry Wireless, a mobile security software company.

LUCY O'DONNELL is the founder of Lovedean Granola, the UK's first manufacturer of granola products.

JEFFREY O'ROURKE is co-founder of eSubstance and now CEO of Ink Publishing, the world's largest producer of in-flight media, with 40+ magazines and clients in 5 continents. Ink Publishing was formed out of a merger of eSubstance and Ink.

MATTHEW PAGE is an old friend, ex-army estate agent and now manager of rock band Feeder.

WILLIAM REEVE is founder and former CEO of LOVEFiLM, Europe's leading online DVD rental subscription service, with over 1 million members and a turnover of £100m. William is ex-McKinsey and a serial entrepreneur.

ROLAND RUDD is an FT journalist and founder of Finsbury Communications, started in 1995 and sold to WPP in 2007. Finsbury provides global financial communications to large companies (25% of the FTSE) and Euro 300. Roland had a remarkable gift of the gab at Oxford and in the Oxford Union, which I admired even then, long before the CEOs of many companies!

VAUGHAN SMITH is a war cameraman, journalist and founder of the Frontline Club, a hospitality and media organisation that supports independent journalism by promoting food, beverages and food for thought. I share Vaughan's interest in foreign news. He is a tough and committed entrepreneur.

NICK WHEELER is founder of Charles Tyrwhitt shirts, a hugely successful multi-channel retailer of quality shirts, ties and suits. Nick has brilliant tenacity and focus.

OTHER REFERENCES

ICOMERA: A Swedish software company that was the first business in the world to put wireless Internet access on public trains.

THIRD SPACE GYM: A comprehensive gym and medical centre in London.

YOU WISH: The world's first free concierge for services.

YOU WISH GROUP: A provider of innovative digital services to large organisations.

Acknowledgements

I want to thank the following people without whom this book would not have happened:

Firstly Sam Jackson at Pearson for steering me through the fascinating process of writing a book, with humour and patience.

Secondly I want to thank all the amazing entrepreneurs who I mention in this book, who have provided so much insight and honesty. The list includes Bill Gross, John Bates, Roland Rudd, Hugo Dixon, Seb James, Janie Brown, Jo Fairley, Jeffrey O'Rourke, Ingrid Murray, Lucy O'Donnell, Peter Christiansen, Victoria Baillieu, Matthew Page, Sue van Meeteren, Greg Hadfield, Nick Wheeler, Matt Norton, Claire Mason, Vaughan Smith, Geoffrey Gestetner, Mark de Wesselow and William Reeve.

Part 1
Prepare for battle

THIS IS THE MOST EXCITING PHASE IN THE
WHOLE JOURNEY — GETTING READY TO GO.

The temptation is to gloss over the detail and focus on the big idea. But there are some basics that you need to get right. There are things that you will have ignored or underestimated. And many of these will be the softer, more emotive issues.

- Who are you doing this with? Are they really a good choice? Have you really thought through whether you have complementary skills and whether you have all the skills that you need? There's no point starting until you do.

- OK so you love the idea, but is it really going to make a good business?

- Can you actually explain what you are doing to a mate in the pub? Does he or she understand it? Does it make a good story? If you can't tell an exciting story then you may not be ready.

- Yes it's going to be a success. I know you believe that. But have you really thought what you'll need to give up to make it work? It won't be plain sailing. Have you properly thought through what you are happy to sacrifice, whether it's money or your love life or your friends? Seriously, something will get sacrificed. Maybe more than one thing. Do you know what it is?

- Is your emotional tank full? Are you ready to take this strain? It will be bloody stressful.

You need to see this as a military operation. You need to prepare properly. You need all your kit to be ready for battle. There's no point getting out there and finding out you forgot the map.

And the first step is to work out who's in it with you and whether other people think they are a good match for you. This is like getting married. You need to take it seriously. Once you start it's hard to separate.

Chapter 1 Blood brothers

In any start-up you need a 'business spouse' – someone who will share the pain with you. This can't be an employee. They need to be a partner with genuine 'skin in the game'. It's easy to be gung-ho when you first have the idea and you are in the early days, but it's rare to find entrepreneurs who can survive without a solid support system in place as the business unfolds. Most of the time this support system comes from their business partners.

But the problem is that often people end up with a business partner, rather than specifically choosing one. For some reason people take less time thinking about who the right partner is for their business and more time thinking about what the business is or isn't. Yet the most critical decision in any start-up involves people.

People make or break a business. That's why investors and VCs focus so hard on the management team.

So don't fall for the trap of not thinking long and hard about your business partners. It just stokes up trouble for the future.

I am a founding non-executive director of Ink, or eSubstance as it was once called, which is now the world's largest producer of in-flight media. It started with a very different business model and team to the one that became so successful. Jeffrey O'Rourke, its CEO and the originator of the idea, explained that 'most people were just people I knew. I met and chose the people who seemed functionally right. Later on, when the business didn't work, we had a much more difficult situation.' In fact, of the original executive team of five people, only two survived. The other three just weren't the right people for the business. One was too corporate. Two had the wrong skills and interests for the eventual business. Insufficient time was spent on getting the right people. You have to be brutal with yourself about the right mix of skills. You need to take more time getting the right people than anything else.

Hugo Dixon, who founded Breakingviews in 1999 with Jonathan Ford, said 'the most important mistake we made was not getting the right commercial people on board. It was a primal sin. We were both editorial and we didn't have commercial or managerial skills. It took many many years to get a team together that I was really happy with on the commercial side.'

> Don't fall for the trap of not thinking long and hard about your business partners. It just stokes up trouble for the future.

In 2003 Vaughan Smith and I were planning to create a new global online broadcaster championing independent cameramen, On The Frontline. Vaughan was an ex-army war cameraman, and founder of Frontline TV, a group of freelance cameramen who supplied the TV industry with their footage from frontlines all over the world. We were high on belief and dreams. I understood the web and he understood foreign journalism. In the end Vaughan created a successful media club, the Frontline Club, but we didn't crack becoming an online broadcaster. With hindsight, Vaughan had to focus elsewhere. He had mortgaged his family home to create the Frontline Club and anything else was going to take a very backseat role. He couldn't do two things at once. He had a massive task to do, just to get the club going. The partnership was bound to be unequal because I could afford to put more time in and deliver my side much more easily than Vaughan. There was a lack of clarity about the business relationship from the start. We just never discussed it properly. In the end I think we both felt that the other person didn't deliver their side of the bargain. We both screwed up.

In most relationships there is often a dominant partner. And this is true of business relationships. The key to making this work is understanding this from the start – knowing who is boss and making sure this is acceptable to everyone concerned.

Nick Velody was a founding director of Joshua, the integrated marketing agency and previously a director at Grey and Ogilvy. Nick is my business partner in You Wish. He and I work well together because it was agreed up front that I was the boss. But it is important to respect that we are also partners and, for things to work, I must listen to and respect his views.

One of the other reasons Vaughan Smith and I also couldn't make our relationship work was because we both wanted to be boss. Ultimately you need a process for decision making and recognition of how that will work. Somebody, the boss, needs to make the final decision. Vaughan and I didn't discuss this issue enough. It meant that we didn't progress as much as we should have done as we weren't shooting in the same direction. The trouble is you don't get to be a successful war cameraman by taking too many orders from other people. You trust your own judgement above anyone else.

Both Mark de Wesselow and Simon White, founders of Square Meal, the successful restaurant, event and drink information publishers, said that trust had been critical to their success. But Mark also said that complementary skills were critical – 'we know each other well which means there's a body of trust, but we have very complementary skills, too. Simon is more numbers focused and I have a feel for the editorial. It's been a good choice.'

Complementary skills is a theme of many successful start-ups. Greg Hadfield, the former

Sunday Times news editor, who founded the website Soccernet, which was sold to ESPN for $40m in 1999, and then Schoolsnet, which was sold to Hotcourses in 2003, believes it is critical. Greg started Soccernet with his 12-year-old son, Tom, in 1995 after taking voluntary redundancy in 1994 and then having got a job on the *Daily Mail* as an investigative journalist with his own web connection. 'There's no way I would have started Soccernet if I didn't have Tom. I had never really looked at the Internet. There's no way Tom would have started it without the *Daily Mail*, the relationship which I brought to the table.' It was an unusual pairing for a start-up – a father and his teenage son – but it worked because trust was there and they both did different things.

> You need a process for decision making and recognition of how that will work. Somebody, the boss, needs to make the final decision.

Matt Norton, co-founder of Sentry Wireless, a mobile security software company, agrees that complementary skills are critical. His partner Ciaran Bradley provides the technology expertise and Matt provides the commercial and sales skills. But he also emphasises two other important points: 'You need overlapping skills to communicate and you need similar lifestyle demands – the same commitments. If they're very different you can't support each other in the same way.'

If you think you're making the wrong choice, then it's crucial you stop and reflect – if you go on the repercussions further down the line could be far greater than pulling out early on.

Sue van Meeteren, who co-founded Jigsaw, a

medium-sized market research agency, said that she resigned from Research International (RI) to start an agency, but then went back to her old company only to resign again two years later and start with different business partners. She said 'Ann and Jo and I all knew each other very well at RI. We knew we were aligned in terms of personality. But I was originally looking to do it with two people who were colleagues and not friends. However, in the end, I felt more comfortable going into business with friends who shared the same values.' And it worked – Jigsaw has become a very successful mid-sized agency, with a turnover of £6m and offices in London and Amsterdam.

But you don't want to let everything rest on trust. It's important to get something legally binding in place too and a contract is the best way to do this. Do not let people tell you that they'll sort out the contract in due course. No. Contracts are too important to be left to the vagaries of new-found friendship. I remember being stiffed by someone when I became the junior partner, with a minority equity stake. I swallowed the friendly line that it would all be sorted out on paper in due course. But obviously it wasn't. And later when it finally was sorted out I ended up with less than I had expected and this was more heavily diluted than we had agreed. My equity percentage was not out of the original 100% but out of 130%, because lots of other people were involved by then!

It's much the same with personal relationships.

> You don't want to let everything rest on trust. It's important to get something legally binding in place too.

Both sides make it work. In truth everyone signs up to a mutual agreement, a pact to do their bit to make it work. And it can be surprising how some business partnerships do work. Ink Publishing now has four very strong-minded executive directors. Sometimes I marvel that their relationship works at all, and yet somehow they all balance each other out and whilst they have their disagreements, they all deliver their own work patch very well and so keep a mutual bargain going. As long as the rules of engagement are clear and people deliver what they say they will, disparate groups of people can work well together. And the more they succeed the better it seems to gel.

Finally it is worth remembering that it can be difficult to be partners with your family. Ingrid Murray, a serial entrepreneur, on the founding team of Inspop which became Confused.com, co-founder of Ninah Consulting, which was sold to ZenithOptimedia, and now founder of online supermarket WeBuyNearby, explained 'My sister, Sara (Murray), chose me to start up Ninah Consulting. She needed someone she could trust and someone who could provide marketing expertise. We complemented each other well and brought different skills. But it's difficult working with family or friends – you have to set the ground rules. Sara would come round on Sunday for lunch and want to talk about work. I wanted her to be a sister not my business partner. We worked together for seven years. It took a few years after not working together to get that back.

Although blood is thicker than water, when you see a person in business you see a side of them you may not want to see. You don't deal with it at the time. You do what you have to do. I really admire family businesses that make it work.'

John Bates, Adjunct Professor of Entrepreneurship, London Business School and entrepreneur says 'never go into business with friends unless you're prepared to lose them. Even long-lasting friendships may break down.'

Here are some basics that you need to get right when choosing business partners:

1 Agree what you expect out of each other, specifically and thoroughly. It doesn't matter if you bring different things to the party and don't contribute equally. But what is crucial is that you both know and accept what the other person is doing and is going to do, especially if you do have different lifestyle demands.

2 Work out who the boss is up front and why. Don't duck this issue. Somebody will need to make decisions and all sides need to be comfortable with that. You can't assume that you will work it out as you go along.

3 Look at what skills you have in the team. Do you and your partner have complementary skills? Does the partnership have what is required? You have to be very objective about this even if time has passed and you are all committed. It's better to jump out of the boat when it's still at the dock rather than when you're far out to sea! If you don't have the right combination, then add other people as you go along, even as non-executives. Check with outsiders as to whether you have the right team and whether there are any gaps.

4 Make it legal. Yes it's 80% trust, but never take the other side purely on trust. If there is mutual trust then there should be no problem in putting it into writing. Many entrepreneurs hate making a commitment and want to be able to zig and zag all the time. That is fine if you are an outsider or a contractor or a potential employee, but once you are both on board then life can't work like that. This is particularly true of anything to do with money. You have to put points that relate to remuneration down on paper.

5 Plan for disaster as well as for success. Then no-one can complain later. In most businesses not all the original founders stay on board. Some will leave along the way – sometimes happily and sometimes unhappily. This is why you need to think through each possible scenario. I have seen some people leave new start-ups remarkably early with a small equity stake which later makes them a lot of money and I have seen others leave acrimoniously without a fair deal. It wastes a lot of time and energy when it goes wrong and no-one has thought about it up front.

6 Get the respective personal partners on board, whether this is the husband, wife, girlfriend or boyfriend. If they feel isolated or pissed off then it will put another significant stress on the business and you don't need that.

Chapter 2
Genius or madness

HOW DO YOU KNOW WHEN THE IDEA IS RIGHT?

'We can all be Dragons when we judge other people's businesses, but it's much harder to do it to your own business. It sounds obvious but it's easy to be obsessed with the idea and not the money. And you only really know whether the idea is any good when you start making a profit. It's just that simple.'

said Peter Christiansen, a media entrepreneur, business school partner and friend, as we drank a glass of wine and talked about our latest ventures. Peter had successfully built a $20m TV production company, Zeal Television, and Speedshape, a high-end computer graphics producer to the advertising industry.

And here I was investing in building a new business that wouldn't make any money until I had spent quite a lot!

'Good ideas make money. You need to sell something people want to buy. If there isn't demand, it's a bad idea,' he continued.

'But lots of ideas need investment to get off the ground – so what then?' I enquired.

'Well then you need to raise some money. If you can't raise the money then it's a lousy idea. The labour of love does not work.'

So how do you know if your idea is any good, if it takes time to set up? It may be technology that needs building or a plant that needs investment, for example. The truth is, you don't. You can do tons of market research, and it does help to some extent, but, in the end, only when it makes a profit do you know for sure. The process of starting a new business is enough to drive you mad. Whilst you may believe that it is a genius idea, it could be bloody daft.

> The process of starting a new business is enough to drive you mad. Whilst you may believe that it is a genius idea, it could be bloody daft.

Jeffrey O'Rourke, CEO of Ink, says: 'You'll never get there if you're swimming against the tide. If you're on the right wave then it's hard to do anything wrong.' This might be a business trend, a technology, an emerging market or the impact of regulatory change.

You also need a simple but compelling insight. Hugo Dixon said about Breakingviews: 'We had a good idea. The Internet meant that you didn't have to wait until tomorrow to get your insight, you could get it today. In financial markets time really makes a difference. We were the first people to provide immediate insight.'

But William Reeve, founder of LOVEFiLM, an online DVD rental business, stresses the absolute financial imperative, especially in a competitive market, even if it takes time to work it out: 'I measure any business idea in terms of the economic model and metrics to show that it can be done. I need to know that the business will survive and that it's just a case of managing the metrics to get there. I liked the Netflix idea of renting DVDs by post. But it took 12 months to work out a plan for doing it in the UK because there were four people already in the space. I couldn't find a way in. It needed money and more than I had.'

Talking to fellow entrepreneurs is often a quick way to get an immediate barometer reading on whether your idea is going to make a good business and whether there is a real market for it.

You Wish was a simple idea. It was the world's first free concierge for services. It helps busy people find services without doing all the searching and helps companies find customers without advertising. It just turns the traditional selling model on its head. You state what you want and who you are, and companies respond personally if they're interested. It saves you time and effort, and it saves businesses time and money because they don't have to pay to find you, they can just concentrate on giving you what you want.

People could see the potential of the idea. Everybody I knew could relate to the problem of insufficient time to look for services like lawyers, podiatrists, venues or cleaners and that long wish list of services we want that we all carry around. And businesses liked it. It was a no brainer. 'Reverse search' was how people summed it up.

But the looming question was: 'Is it a pain killer or just a vitamin pill? Pain killers make money. Vitamins often don't!'

If so many people said it was good, then why did it feel so risky?

Well, I had to build an online platform and then attract two different customer audiences – simultaneously. It's a big challenge to turn supply and demand on their head and effing hard to carry it off. It needs a partnership. It needs investment. I could get the idea some of the way, but not the whole way. That's scary. I could be so close and yet in danger of running out of money. Or I could overspend on the basis of my self-belief and find out too late that I was wrong!

As it turned out, I was half right. Online lead generation was a good market, but a different business model was needed.

I have had plenty of ideas throughout my life – a fashion label, nightclubs, an online news broadcaster, a theme park (that is still genius, it just needs a few £billion!) and a new marketing agency. Some have been on my own, and some with others – including Utterly Butterly, that great buttery spread! Some of these have been good ideas but some were bonkers. The more ideas you have and the more you seriously try them out, the better you get.

The excitement of a new idea is awesome. The idea that you can create something new, innovative, valuable and loved – something that solves a problem or brings pleasure – is wild. When that idea pops up it's like a new toy, an

The excitement of a new idea is awesome. The idea that you can create something new, innovative, valuable and loved is wild.

obsession. It's something that needs to fly or be given birth to. It's a Rocky Horror Picture Show moment. As Dr. Frank-N-Furter would say about his creation, Rocky, he had discovered the 'secret to life itself'. It's very personal. It's yours. You made it …

The trouble is, although it may be genius to you, it's a waste of time if it doesn't mean anything to anyone else! The trick here is learning impartiality when you listen to other people. If people don't get it or reject it, it kills you. You don't know whether it means you are mad or they are wrong. It's hard to stay objective. It can be very depressing.

Often the problem is that you haven't found a way of executing and communicating it properly so that people really see and believe in it. People are creatures of habit and one of the simplest ways of dealing with that is to reference precedents for the idea. If they can relate it to something they understand you're half way there.

It is also important to be very clear about whether you want to create something new and different or just something better. As Nick Wheeler, founder of Charles Tyrwhitt shirts in 1986 and now with a turnover of £60m, said: 'It wasn't the idea – it was about doing it better. The idea wasn't the issue. The vast majority of businesses are trying to be different. People say they can't start a business because they don't have an idea. They don't need a new idea!'

But timing can also play a critical role, as Bill Gross of Idealab explained: 'We have ideas that are too early; maybe five or ten years too early. There is a tendency when the idea isn't working to say "let's market it harder", but often the reverse is true. Just survive on less. The lesson is don't be in a rush. Either find a way to survive until the market takes off or get out. The tendency is to do a Hail Mary. Instead a slow and steady can be a valuable strategy.'

The good news is that there are some practical steps that you can follow to help you gauge whether you have a good idea or not, whether better or different and whether the timing is right. The faster you follow some of these points, the faster you will get to know the answer.

1 Trust your own instincts. Do you have doubts? If so listen to them and rework the idea until those doubts go away. I know from my own experience that even if I can answer the key questions, I have moments of doubt. It's in these moments I can see that there are points that I have not dealt with – if I addressed these points I could move the idea forward. Eventually you will work most of the doubts away. You may always have some, but if you have a good idea then you will eventually work through most of them.

2 Can you describe your idea in one sentence to someone you have never met in the pub? If you are struggling to do this then you may not be there yet.

3 Can a proven business person play back the business opportunity to you or do they give you too many reasons why not?

4 Understand that you never finish the idea – it evolves, it lives. Go with the idea. See it as tidal movement. You can't control every moment of it. Indeed you would not want to. As with nature, there are times in the emergence of a new idea when the tide takes you somewhere unexpected but somehow it is a better place. Learn to live with this ebb and flow. It is sometimes two steps forward and one back but then that is the passion, the journey of life and of the entrepreneur. Who would give it up?!

5 Keep asking people and testing. Success is the world around you. If they vouch for its success, then you know that you are on to a winner. Until then keep reformulating that cake mix. It will come good and if it doesn't then learn from it and go again.

Chapter 3 Telling stories

'You're a bloody fool. You'll get yourself killed in Afghanistan and for what? For people who don't care about what you're trying to do for them and who are as bloodthirsty as they always were.' My dad was furious and in despair.

I had dreamt up the idea of the Oxford Afghanistan Expedition in 1986. The goal was to film and report on the forgotten war that was going on in Afghanistan. Possibly my first ever pitch for a new idea was therefore to Sandy Gall, seasoned journalist and broadcaster at ITN. He was deeply and probably rightfully sceptical, and advised that this was no game for amateurs. It didn't win me any camera equipment out of ITN, but it didn't put me off. Eventually a fellow student, Radek Sikorski, and I raised £5000 to fund it and ended up joining the mujahideen in August as we headed off to film the war. Later Radek was the first foreign journalist to photograph Stinger missiles in action and I had moved on to my first serious job.

Some business ideas are pure genius as soon as they emerge, and are immediately fundable. They have a simple idea at their core that has clear appeal to a specific customer group and is monetisable. But most aren't. They need rework and then more rework and even then, most of these never get funded and die.

Why?

Because the story isn't right.

Telling stories is a critical asset for entrepreneurs in their quest to get this funding. But the other oft forgotten benefit of storytelling is that it provides the entrepreneur with invisible armour. This armour protects against the inevitable blows of non-believers, who think you are stark staring mad – why would you be taking such high risks, when you could be earning a decent wage and getting down to the pub at an early hour? Surviving the scepticism of friends and family is tougher than coping with scepticism from strangers. It drips away in your mind at all hours. Having a story to tell – something unexpected, insightful and compelling – can change this dynamic. It can help you wrestle through when things are feeling rather bleak.

Some people are born natural storytellers, but most of us are not and have to learn. And as always, the more you do it the better you get.

The dotcom boom ten years on provided another world of storytelling. Most people

> Telling stories is a critical asset for entrepreneurs in their quest to get funding.

thought I was mad to be involved in the web. My mother used to say that she wished I had stayed in advertising, 'where you were doing so well, darling'! But I told her that the Internet was the future and that if WPP, a titan of marketing globally, was prepared to invest in us when we were so young and tiny, then it was only a matter of time before we created something really big. Just one success was the start point of the story. You can then grow it from there – success by success. It could be winning another client or creating an industry first. You build it layer by layer, with each extra layer reinforcing the first one.

One day later, in 1999 at a board meeting, we finally took the decision to float syzygy, our digital agency, and crafted our story around three simple but powerful points. We were profitable and most dotcom companies weren't. We had built a pan-European business in the three largest markets in Europe and most companies hadn't. We had strong expertise in enduring industry sectors.

By the time I was standing as CEO of syzygy in the German Stock Exchange on 6 October 2000, we had constructed an awesome story that had seen our roadshow oversubscribed by 15 times. We were valued at €240m. It was amazing how the story got better and better the more we crafted it.

A few years later I'm now back on the road again with a new business. It's taken a year to formulate and now it's out there. The same pain as before. How do you get the message across properly? How do you stop yourself screaming when a friend says 'I don't get it'? How many times do I have to rewrite that bloody executive summary and still find that it has not captured the story right? It's amazing how some days you just feel like staying at home because you can't get the pitch right. But you just need to keep doing it and refining it and learning from it. You have to soak up the comments. You have to make every criticism a moment of joy, another lesson learnt for free.

When I took the You Wish proposition to the first potential investor and he told me that it was at far too early a stage to invest, I wasn't surprised – most VCs don't do very early stage these days. But when he also commented on the dependency on expensive arbitrage in the business model, I had to reflect and use this to revise my story, rather than disagree! The story wasn't convincing enough. The way You Wish made money depended on the need for too many customers without an easy and affordable way to get them. The story had to be revised.

The next VC I approached was a personal friend and who thought the idea was 'very interesting' but then went on to say 'don't waste your money on it'. And so it goes on.

You battle through each criticism and find an answer, a solution that solves the problem. Each time you add weight to the story. This is the nature of the game. You have to make it foolproof.

Slowly and surely your storytelling will start to work and the feeling is incredible.

Slowly and surely your storytelling will start to work and the feeling is incredible. I went to meet up with the ex-CEO of a very large branded retailer. I was pissed off. Our product was still not right and the timing plan was slipping and the whole bloody thing was taking too long. I rehearsed the story and the arguments as I went to meet him. It took ages to order the coffee but finally we started, sitting quietly in the street outside Caffè Nero. And he loved it. He really loved the concept – the story! For one hour and a half it's intense. You are 100% focused on talking about your baby. You put as much passion and conviction as you can into the argument. Christ, a really senior business man is considering how he could help grow it.

'Why are you only going for £800k? I thought you would say £10million. This could be huge if you align it to a big consumer brand with millions of customers. Between us I am sure that we could call a few people and raise that money in four hours' he said.

Blimey, wouldn't I like to believe that? Mind you, I can't show the fact that I am running out of money, I thought to myself, and said, under my breath, 'Yes I have got enough money. It's just a case of keeping it going until I find the right partner.' He had identified the solution to the weakness that the earlier investor had pointed out – get a large and trusted corporate partner on board.

I finally leave and am so fizzed up that I walk for an hour just enjoying the spring day as darkness descends. I cancel the curry with the boys as I can't afford to get pissed now. I need to reflect on this and anyway I would probably go mental. Not now, not yet …

And it's important to construct an interesting and PR'able story to share with a wider range of people and create a groundswell of interest. Jo Fairley of Green & Black's was a former journalist and has a real eye for a storyline. She got this just right with Green & Black's. It wasn't just a delicious new chocolate. It was a product sourced directly from the farmers in Belize and the Dominican Republic, who were guaranteed a fair price for their crop. It was Fairtrade chocolate. As she says, 'The heart of the story was seeing the truth of the impact of the business on a Third World community. Quite often, aid doesn't get to where it is meant to be. When you trade with a community, you can see the impact and how they advance themselves with the resources you give. It was crucial to tell that story. My first press release picked this up: "Guilt free chocolate? Well almost". This was a great story with many interesting layers to it.'

As everybody tells you, investors buy people and you need to show commitment and passion. Vaughan put his passion into setting up the Frontline Club as a 'living camp fire' for the fallen cameramen and women who put their lives on the line to bring news back to others. His unbelievable commitment, hard work and skill helped get the support of many people that has helped fan the flames of his endeavour. As he said 'It was the story that existed that enabled this business to happen. The story is crucial to success. Our story is our reputation.'

Bill Gross, founder and CEO of Idealab, an incubator in California which founded eToys, Citysearch, CarsDirect, Cooking.com, FreePC, Tickets.com and GoTo.com, believes that 'If an entrepreneur isn't in love with the product, then the company is destined to fail. Every business you look at, it falls on hard times. The only way to survive is to be passionate. If I wasn't in love with it, then I would give it up. In fact if you're not in love then give it up.'

You also need conviction, as Matthew Page, the manager of rock band Feeder, says: 'You can't be sheepish. You'll never sell anything!'

But passion is often not enough. Vaughan and I had a lot of passion when we tried to raise money to launch the online news broadcaster at the very early stages of video on the web. Through our drive we assembled a very strong team of the great and good in news and current affairs, but ultimately the business model did not appear sound to potential investors – we'd spent too much time on the story and neglected other crucial ingredients.

And, finally, you do need to be clear on who your audience is and what they need to hear. I remember once being in the final part of the selection process for the Conservative Party's prospective Parliamentary candidate for Hillingdon in 2004. I had to make a three-minute speech as to why I was the right

> You also need conviction, as Matthew Page, the manager of rock band Feeder, says: 'You can't be sheepish. You'll never sell anything!'

candidate. I started with an impassioned plea for the Conservative value, freedom. I explained how I had joined the mujahideen in the 80s to help free the Afghan people from Soviet tyranny, but was rapidly interrupted by a lady asking me whether I was a member of al-Qaeda.

It killed my selection chances stone dead!

Most successful serial entrepreneurs weave a story that combines magic, product, people and money in one. A perfect concoction for their audience. Too often an entrepreneur can have some of these, but not all four.

So how do you create a compelling, convincing and memorable story?

1 Recognise that this is a long game. It's not one pitch, it's *every* day. It's your life story until you get to the finish line. It's a marathon. You have to get good at it. You have to practise. It took nine months to start and complete our IPO roadshow presentation for syzygy. You are going to have bad days as well as good days while you craft it. It has to be a natural, simple but compelling story.

2 You have to have conviction. You have to understand all sides of the argument – the pros and the cons – and be prepared to work through the answers and take the time to convince your audience. You need to learn from the doubters. You have to believe your story absolutely.

3 It's got to be simple. You have to link the problem you are solving to a better solution and the right team to deliver it. Then you need to wrap that up in some examples of early success.

4 You have to relish the chance to tell the story. If you don't then you can't expect your potential investors to like what you have to say. You need to be able to excite people on the bus or in the board room.

5 You need to demonstrate your personal commitment. Have you sacrificed something to get here? How can you demonstrate that?

6 Always have a piece of new news. Always impress people with your activity, your achievements. This is what creates momentum and belief. People always marvel at the speed and agility of successful entrepreneurs. So behave like one.

WHAT MAKES A GOOD ENTREPRENEURIAL STORY?

1. Be clear on who your audience is and what they need to hear, and not just what you want to tell them.
2. Develop one simple hook to engage with their beliefs, desires and needs. Keep it really simple.
3. Find everyday illustrations of how you will deliver value throughout your story.
4. Give them passion. Make them see your unrelenting conviction. They're buying you after all.

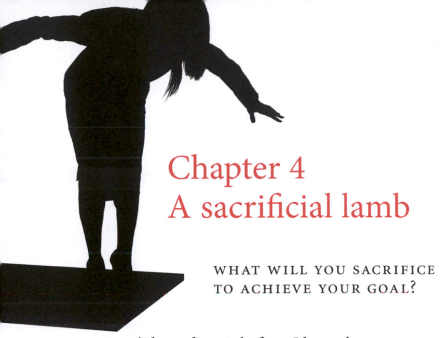

Chapter 4
A sacrificial lamb

WHAT WILL YOU SACRIFICE
TO ACHIEVE YOUR GOAL?

'I have done it before. I know how to start a business. I know what I need to do,' I said to Patrick in a supremely confident way as we sipped cold lagers in the setting sun near our opulent offices in Mayfair.

But thinking about it ten months later when I was no longer on someone else's payroll in Mayfair, had I really thought it through properly?

Well, yes, of course, I had worked out what money I was prepared to spend. I was intending to use the money that my father left me, when he died. So that's that then.

No it bloody well shouldn't be. This requires a very careful and thoughtful review of your 'life's assets' to work out which ones you are prepared to sacrifice and which ones you aren't.

Ages ago when I started another business, I hadn't thought about anything. I hadn't anticipated the impact of not having a salary, not in terms of the money, but in terms of my self-esteem. We all build our confidence on the basis of praise and the value that others attribute to us. When you strip this away, there's no-one to praise you, do your review, promote you and pay you more money at the end of the month. This can have a surprisingly destructive effect on you unless you are really ready for it.

To test whether you're ready, you need to run your own life audit; it's a careful assessment of three key areas of your life.

Firstly, is your new start-up in line with your own passions and strengths? Is it something that you love doing and really care about? When the going gets tough, will you still care enough about it to keep going? You need to be really clear that this is part of your life's work. If you don't care much about it then do something else, or invest some money in someone else who does.

As Mark de Wesselow, founder of Square Meal, said: 'I had expected a bit of hard work, but what I didn't expect was for people's attitudes to something innovative to be as closed or negative as they sometimes were. It can take a long time to persuade people to get on board. You need to have belief in it. This can't be overstated enough. You need to know what you're letting yourself in for. What you also don't realise until you start is that you feel quite exposed. You feel you are being watched. Lots of friends and family know. You have to justify your existence. This can lead to a bit of a bunker mentality.'

Secondly, what assets do you have, whether

> To test whether you're ready, you need to run your own life audit.

physical, intellectual, emotional or indeed spiritual? Consider a full inventory of those assets including your money (cash, equities, investments and pensions), your home, your health, your job, your happiness, your marriage/relationship/love, your family, your self-confidence and last but by no means least your time. Which of these do you care most about and which are you prepared to sacrifice? It may sound odd to consider sacrificing anything when you haven't even started on your killer business, especially when you are so fired up about it, but it's worth it. Some entrepreneurs find it easy to sacrifice other people, their friends and family as they focus all their time on their baby. Others are quite happy to throw their cash at their idea but won't sacrifice their free time. You need to reflect on what matters most and what doesn't. You need to recognise that people close to you will also be forced to make sacrifices, for you, like going on holidays together. Once you've started, you will lose control. No matter how good they are, most people do lose control – at least for a while.

As John Bates, Adjunct Professor of Entrepreneurship, London Business School and entrepreneur, says: 'Starting a business is like starting a love affair. It is exclusive and intense. The partner doesn't get a look in. You sacrifice freedom – you are simply not free. You are at the behest of the business 24/7.'

Thirdly, what lifestyle do you need to lead to be happy? Do you need holidays every three months and weekends away? Do you need to be having fun and socialising with people? Or do you need security? Some people have become so accustomed to corporate fuelled lifestyles that they find it hard to live without them. If you can't, then make sure you pick a start-up business that makes money from Day 1. Most start-ups don't. That may mean you can't have your holiday and more.

As Jeffrey O'Rourke of Ink said: 'I expected to work long hours. I expected it would give me control over my time but actually I feel the company has control of my time. There is no separation between work and home.'

Are you ready for that? It won't necessarily give you exactly what you want or hope for.

And sometimes it will take you a while to get there, as Geoffrey Gestetner of Cistermiser said: 'To get into the position I am in, I spent a long time working away from home in my twenties and lost some of my personal life. It was then tough looking for a business to buy, but I had no mortgage and no family. It took two and a half years to find the business!'

And sometimes there are a more complicated set of choices, according to Ingrid Murray: 'I have got this idea [WeBuyNearby] but I am a single mum with four boys. Super mum here thinks I can start the business and be a single mum. You don't think through the reality. Most people struggle to be a mum of two kids. So now my ex-husband is moving down here again to help. But my partner of six months is now wondering whether he will see much of me. Will the relationship survive? You have to think through these issues before they run into you!'

The more times I start businesses the better I become at following some of these basic guidelines. I try to feel instinctively whether it is in line with my passions and strengths. I have also become much more comfortable with working out in advance what assets I will sacrifice without regret. But I always underestimate the impact it will have on my lifestyle, on having fun and taking time out. I guess it's like playing against great Mahjong or Risk players. They really do have thought-out strategies based on years of experience, analysis and watching other masters at work. They don't do half the preparation. They don't protect a country at the expense of a continent. They don't spread themselves too thin. They have a plan. When they attack they come in force.

In addition it helps to manage your risk – the potential sacrifice. As Matt Norton of Sentry Wireless said: 'It's a calculated risk. I am not a big risk taker. At the time I looked at trying to negate the risks. I took out an extra mortgage and put the money aside. I thought I could always get another job. I resisted the temptation of Belinda (my wife) throwing in her job. She is working like a Trojan in order that we have semblance of stability. It was a big decision, but calculated.'

> You need to be composed about and prepared for what might happen – the positives and the negatives.

Finally you need to be composed about and prepared for what might happen – the positives and the negatives. As Seb James, an entrepreneur who co-founded Silverscreen, a VC-backed DVD retailer, and now a director at retailer Dixons (DSGI) said: 'You need to start from the premise that it will be OK. Not everything you have is necessary. Then you can be more serene.'

So how do you prepare yourself for this potential sacrifice?

1 You must recognise that you will sacrifice something. Everybody does. I don't mean sacrificing a safe salary or a 9–5 job or a guaranteed state pension. This is obviously the case, albeit a very scary one for some people. No it means other things, such as your money or your relationships or your health. All of these things get thrown on to the funeral pyre by people desperate to make their dreams work. You may be lucky but most people suffer something. If you recognise it up front it will make you think more rationally about it and help you make better choices.

2 Choose what you won't sacrifice under any situation and preserve it. If you know that there are certain things that you won't sacrifice, then it takes away any uncertainty or prevarication as you are swept up in the whole event. If you are prepared to sacrifice health and money then don't throw your marriage away at the same time – work on that one instead!

3 Get permission from your loved ones in advance to do this. You need them to be on your side. They need to understand what you are going to sacrifice and be comfortable with that. You may choose to ignore them but at least you know their views.

4 Encourage others around you to get some other reward while you are focused on your thing. Don't let them and your relationships wither on the vine. Make sure that they are emotionally satisfied in some other way as you are likely to deprive them of much attention or love.

5 Have a contingency plan. It will take twice as much time as you expected. You will spend more money than you envisaged. You will need to bootstrap your way forward, ducking and diving to get what you want. So you need some form of risk management. Why not consider staying in your current workplace on a part-time basis? Or maybe they will value your time in some other way to help pay the bills?

6 Listen to what people tell you will be the biggest challenges and seek to find mitigations to them in advance. Think through all the likely scenarios so that you have an idea of what to expect and how to behave if they happen.

HOW DO YOU KEEP YOUR HUSBAND OR WIFE OR BOYFRIEND OR GIRLFRIEND ON SIDE?

1. Recognise that you are driving this and you need to keep telling them what is going on. My wife Jo said: 'All you can do is ride the roller coaster with them. You can't steer it. You're just a support. You worry about their lows but also their highs because inevitably they'll come down with a bang!'

2. Agree boundaries. Will you work all the time? Will you help at home at all?

3. Take your agreed time out with your family and friends when you say you will. Don't just push it all back for another time.

4. Try to be honest. As Matt Norton of Sentry Wireless said: 'I may have mis-sold it to Belinda [his wife]. But it wasn't conscious. My optimism blinded me; if only I had delivered half of my first revenue forecast!'

Chapter 5 Bottle the highs to cope with the lows

HOW DO YOU MAKE SURE YOU SEE THE POSITIVES AND NOT JUST THE NEGATIVES?

'I am feeling great about this local channel strategy. It's the key to unlocking everything. It makes such good sense. Both of these couples could be our local agents and both seem interested. I had a three-hour meeting with the second couple last night – they just couldn't stop talking and asking questions,' Nick, my partner at You Wish, said excitedly as we took our tea in Frank's cafe on a sunny Friday morning in London.

My God, I thought, we may finally have cracked the channel strategy. We're going to make this new channel strategy work!

After struggling with our channel strategy for ages, it now looked as though we might have several partners in play. This could boost our chances of getting funding. None of the partnerships were signed in ink yet but they were ongoing and positive discussions and it was time to recognise that this was real progress.

There are moments of pure elation in starting your own business – an amazing sense of power over your own destiny and satisfaction that you don't have to be a wage slave to someone else. And yet all too frequently they are punctuated by moments of doubt, despair and anger. So it's critical to savour those highs because they may shortly be followed by miserable times.

An unfortunate human tendency can be to reflect on the things that you feel you have got wrong, rather than things that have gone right. After all, it's not easy being on your own, without an office support system, without the familiar water cooler conversations, the office flirting or even the inevitable Christmas party! Yet the thing about having your own business is the satisfaction of a job well done, a job conceived by you. This is at the heart of keeping your spirits up and bottling the great moments.

There are a number of ways of doing this. On an individual level and before you start, it can be very valuable to remind yourself of past successes that are relevant to your new venture and to use that as a tool to inspire and uplift yourself. Like the mantra in transcendental meditation, it allows you to centre yourself on

> The thing about having your own business is the satisfaction of a job well done, a job conceived by you.

something positive and stress-relieving. The fact that I floated an earlier business is hugely relevant to my new venture. Not only are they both Internet companies, but they demonstrate my ability to build and execute an exit for shareholders, which is so critical to many potential investors. But I can also picture myself standing proud by the life-size sculpture of the bull outside the Frankfurt Stock Exchange just moments before syzygy actually became a public company. That triumphal vision can help banish negative thoughts – after all, if you can do it once, who says you can't do it again!

You also need to feel ready for the stress that will come. You need to put an invisible cloak of self-belief around yourself. You need to avoid having any other big emotional distractions in your life or anything else that might sap your strength. As Victoria Baillieu, co-founder of Pay Check, a managed payroll business for the private sector, said: 'for me the business changed when I left my husband Danny. There was a massive thing of not failing. Nothing was going to stand in my way to let the business fail, because I felt that I had failed in my marriage.'

And remember the positive reasons why you are doing it. As Jo Fairley of Green & Black's says: 'When I was 16 and on holiday, I bought a postcard of a man on a high diving board with the caption: "If you don't do it, you'll never know what would have happened if you had done it."'

The easiest way to develop the right mindset is to celebrate each hurdle overcome on the journey of your start-up. At syzygy we had an implicit agreement that each year we would take on a client project that was too difficult and new for us to deliver, in order to force the organisation to learn and cope with transformation and change. When we won the project to deliver the first Boots e-commerce site, it was a massive win for us and a hugely challenging task. We got there and the company was much richer for the experience. This is a great mindset to adopt – a relentless pursuit of excellence and corporate self-improvement.

And even this success had a funny story with it, which always makes me smile and think about overcoming adversity. I had taken the whole company of 60 people to Disneyland Paris to celebrate what we had done for Boots, shortly after the shiny new e-commerce site launched. I was on the ice rink when my senior client rang me to say the site had gone down! What could I say, especially because every single syzygy person was in Paris? Luckily a former employee was still working in our office and after our initial panic, we managed to get him to start it up again. What a scare. What a miraculous escape! The joys and excitement of the early days of the web! It's a great story to remember when times are tough.

So with a new start-up, try to celebrate every single key moment in its incarnation. This can begin with something as simple as finding a name for your company. Well I say simple. We changed the name of You Wish four times before arriving at the right name. Every time we thought that we had found a great name, people told us it wasn't any good. And, sadly, on reflection, they were right.

We spent literally hundreds of collective hours trying to crack this problem. It needed to be memorable, work with the core consumer proposition and have an easy website URL and the latter is the most difficult problem, which is why so many start-ups have funny names. Finally Nick, my partner, was on eBay and spotted that www.youwish.com was for sale. It was perfect on all levels. Nick put in the top bid, but that was still way below the asking price so we hadn't got it. We emailed the owner directly in LA. He had been running an adult site, but had now stopped. We weren't sure how straight the guy was, so eventually agreed a price and put the money in escrow and signed. It was ours. Well, it still took weeks to get the URL into our hands and before I stopped being superstitious about whether we would really get it.

Everyone loves the name and it's perfect for what we are doing. That was a huge victory. As with all small businesses, every victory is a step closer to success. It allows you to bottle another good moment rather than always stressing about the bad ones! Mind you, the fact that it was once an adult site meant that all the major search engines had it blacklisted and it took us months to get it whitelisted. Even now it's suffering from low rankings on Google. Fuck, two steps forward and one step backwards!

As with all small businesses, every victory is a step closer to success.

45

When you find a way to create additional value from what you are doing then celebrate. Celebrate that you have been lateral, creative and a bloody genius. When we concluded two partnerships for You Wish that I had never originally envisaged, but that people believed would be real successes, I certainly deserved a pat on the back!

Mark de Wesselow, founder of Square Meal also reiterates this point: 'Write down your goals at the start, so that you can celebrate the achievement moment. The danger is that you are always redefining the goals, so you never say well done, job done. For your own psychology, you need to celebrate little achievements. There is no-one else who will pat you on your back!'

'For your own psychology, you need to celebrate little achievements. There is no-one else who will pat you on your back!'

There is a semi-sequential list of all the key moments in a start-up. It starts with the business idea and getting validation that the opportunity exists. Then there is the name and getting good people. The people may start with the founders but will quickly benefit from having non-executives and advisers. So you have an idea, a team and a company, now you need a product or service that works and customers who love it. Maybe you then need partners to help you deliver and the PR that makes more people aware of it. Then hopefully this starts to generate revenues and then profits. And maybe along the way you need external investment? Celebrating each time you hit one of these milestones is critical to success and keeping morale at a high – which is crucial for when times get, inevitably, tough.

As well as celebrating success, it's equally important to have some fun and laughter along the way. Some of this can be amazingly puerile, but it all breaks the tension as you progress. I remember being in a bar in New York in 1997 when John Hunt and I were looking at whether we should establish an office there. John was the original founder of syzygy and my business partner. He is a serial entrepreneur who started and sold a software company, Obongo, to AOL while I was running syzygy and subsequently started Oriel Wines. We were supposedly talking business with some potential partners when I managed to tuck the skirt of a very pretty girl into the back of her knickers without her noticing. It was just like the famous 70s' poster of the tennis girl scratching her bare bottom! It amused and horrified John in equal measure and always dissolved us into tears long afterwards.

People will tell you to recognise success every day and write it down somewhere as a reminder of what has been achieved. Then you can collect your successes as a vehicle to build a ladder. But it's bullshit. You will never do that. You'll be running around like a headless chicken most of the time!

So what's the real formula for capturing the highs?

1 Use your past successes as a reminder to you and others of how bloody good you are and therefore how good you are going to be. Reflect on those successes and not just the big ones but also the smaller successes that you have had.

2 Make change and experimentation an accepted part of company culture. Nothing is forever. Everything can be improved. Every new idea or angle that you have is another success. That way nothing is ever perceived as a failure and only as a learning point towards your inevitable and eventual success in this venture. This also means that new ideas are always highs. They are always moments of excitement.

3 Remember the hurdles that you have achieved to get where you are. You may still have a lot more but that doesn't mean everything is shit! It means that you have done a brilliant job of overcoming lots of issues that would have stopped many other people.

4 Have a laugh whenever you can.

5 Be clear on your goals so you know when you achieve one.

Part 2
Taking the strain

WHEN YOU START, YOUR SELF-CONFIDENCE HELPS
YOU POWER ON.

It's scary, but it's still really exciting. Now you are making your dream
come true. But there are surprises around every corner and you need
to have a high level of resilience to deal with these early challenges:

- Your product isn't right in spite of all that preparatory work you
  did. How do you deal with people not seeing what you see? How
  do you get it right?

- You are a bit stressed. How do you cope as the stress mounts? What
  can you do to keep it under control?

- You need help. You need to think differently about whom you
  know and how they can help you. You need all the help you can
  get – maybe it's friends, maybe it's acquaintances. Maybe someone
  can mentor you?

- And just when you thought it was safe, you've discovered many
  more competitors than you thought and some of them are doing
  better than you. How do you cope with that?

- And yes you are getting pissed off with your business partners or they're getting pissed off with you. What advice can you get to help you manage these relationships?

The first place you really feel the stress is with your product or service. Is it as well constructed as you thought? Is it making money? More importantly what do other people think? Do people value it?

Chapter 6
Cutting and re-cutting

HOW TO GET YOUR PRODUCT RIGHT

'Chris, I don't get it. I am not sure what I am supposed to do or what to use it for ...'

How can someone sensible say that? Surely it's bleeding obvious what you do?

Well no, actually. If the customer doesn't get it or doesn't like it, then it's our fault not theirs. I was cross that a friend of mine didn't understand what we were trying to do. In fact I was bloody furious. I was angry with him, angry with myself and angry with our product.

It hurts because it's so personal. You have taken hours, weeks, months and even years in some cases, to create something which you believe is viable. It must be right. Well, no actually. The idea may be right on paper but that doesn't mean that the delivery of it is right. It can get rejected in a few minutes, sometimes even a few seconds. 'It's bruuutal!' as an American friend of mine says in her New Jersey accent. The truth is that the Internet and the explosion in communication and technology of the past ten years has made us all 'reviewers'. People power has taken off and anyone daring to put their own new baby on the parapet can get shot down in flames very quickly. Equally the Internet has made it very easy for millions of people to start ideas that may never be good businesses.

There is a fundamental difference between the idea and the product and one should not confuse the two. Many people have ideas, but turning them into great products is another story completely. In the end a product is only good enough when people want to use it and *pay* to do this. Money talks. Someone has to pay for your product somewhere along the line, even if it is a potential business selling to your users. A brilliantly clever idea with no customers is worth nothing.

Part of the pain that you feel in developing the product is that you get too close to it personally.

Part of the pain that you feel in developing the product is that you get too close to it personally and you bring in too many flawed assumptions. This is part of the process. You have to accept it.

I have seen so many good business ideas fail because insufficient time was given to crafting the right product or service. It does take time and money to get it right.

When Vaughan and I were developing our idea for On The Frontline, an online news broadcaster championing the independent

cameraman from around the world, we found
that there was more than one product that
could be developed. It could be great journalism
from the frontline or it could be genuinely
hard-hitting footage from really dangerous
and difficult parts of the world (Tibet, Burma,
Zimbabwe and China). It had the potential to be
an amazing and unique product. We thought it
could be very powerful but actually some people
saw it as 'war porn' and some just saw it as
another news source.

These days you need to live life in beta. Beta is
the traditional name for software that has passed
its internal testing and is now released to the
public for their testing and feedback. Running
a business like this means you assume that your
products and services are never perfect and can
always be improved with usage and experience.
Update and improve is the mantra that you need
to live by.

When we started eSubstance or what became
Ink Publishing, we believed that there was a great
market for companies buying branded content
online. The product was OK, but it wasn't good
enough to achieve the margins that we needed.
In fact there was just too much content already
on the web. It took us time to recognise that. As
CEO Jeffrey O'Rourke said: 'We raised enough
money to hang ourselves on. We figured out that
our business wasn't working. We were quite lucky
to find a business that helped us reconfigure.
We got two people who were critical to success
and we moved to a print model. We essentially

reversed into Ink. This was luck rather than a grand plan. It's hard when you're unestablished. People are very sceptical. You deal with that through enthusiasm and long hours.'

Focus is also an important part of getting your product right. As Hugo Dixon of Breakingviews said: 'At the start we thought we could have a broad range of content, but we became absolutely focused on financial insight only and our revenue model changed – we moved solely to corporate subscriptions. If we had stayed with the other models, we would have gone bust.' Once you find the sweet spot you have to jettison the baggage that didn't work.

Perseverance is also critical to getting the product right. As Lucy O'Donnell, founder of Lovedean Granola, said: 'I am very passionate about my product. I do really believe in the product. People love it. That is key to my success. I have that belief and so I haven't given up. I have assumed that I can overcome the problems. I was making it in my home. It took me 11 months to find a manufacturer. I hassled a food technology guy. I was one of the first people to make granola in the UK – nobody really knew what granola was then (back in 2005). I then found an MD of a factory who said he would help and was great because he did not make us commit to a yearly volume. Instead he just asked that every production would be a certain amount – in my case three tonnes. We did trials – we stayed in the factory till very late at night until we cracked it.'

> Once you find the sweet spot you have to jettison the baggage that didn't work.

Geoffrey Gestetner spent many years in basic industry, working for Hanson, often in what many of his friends considered were rather god-forsaken places. He didn't care. He loved it. He could talk the hind legs off a donkey about showers and shower fittings! And he has a rare passion for manufacturing where most people don't, which has enabled him to buy his own business and successfully build it as he learnt at Hanson. As he said: 'Jane [his wife] has had to pull me out of men's washrooms because I had been studying the urinals!'

And you need to recognise if you only have half the equation and want to grow then other people may need to come on board. Lucy of Lovedean Granola said: 'I needed to balance my ideas with others. I wanted expertise from a similar area to mine. So Angus [Cameron] and Mark Cuddigan from Dormen Foods [Dormen Foods sold nuts to the trade and was bought by food manufacturer, Glisten] came to join me. There were so many parallels with what I was going through and what Angus had done with Dormen's Nuts. One of the toughest decisions I have made is to bring in partners – I was giving away some of my baby, but I knew I had to do that in order to grow the business.'

With You Wish it has taken us much longer to get to the right place than I ever imagined and it has been an incredibly painful process. We have been down many blind alleys with our product. We have had a big vision for the business but in many ways have tried to encapsulate all of this into one launch product, which you can't do. We needed to get the core journey absolutely right before getting clever and the awful truth with Internet products is that it is very easy to create things that are too complex for your audience. People also tell you different things. Consultants and designers all want to give you the perfect answer, but the truth is that you should only listen to the core audience.

And that's the key point, as Seb James of Silverscreen said: 'You don't have to love your product, but you have to love your customer. You have to love them in all their shapes and sizes and deliver to them.'

You have to have real passion to get your product right and the ultimate arbiter is the customer. You have to keep going until the customer tells you it is right. As Nick Wheeler of Charles Tyrwhitt says: 'I want other people to love the product or service. I love it when we get letters from people saying one of our shirts is the best they have ever had or someone in the call centre did a great job.'

And that means having belief, as Matt Norton says of his Sentry Wireless product: 'I don't think it's important to love it but to believe. Don't tell me you can love anti-spam software but I do believe. You have to believe it is of value. It doesn't have to be exciting and make you smile. There's not a lot that's sexy about nappies, but as a father of two, I see their value!'

So how do you deal with the pain of trying to get the product right, of trying to give your customers what they want to pay for? Here are a few crucial guides:

1 Let the customer be the judge and celebrate that fact. Don't panic when they tell you that things aren't working yet. Engage the customer in giving you all the feedback that you need.

2 Spend time executing your product and iterating it. Understand that you won't get it right first time and maybe even the tenth time, but it will get closer. Follow the view that the Internet has encouraged, which is that the product is never right. Assume that the product is permanently in beta and can always be improved.

3 Recognise early on that someone needs to buy your product. If you can't get them to pay for it, then you don't have a proper product and it will never fly or you need to change your business model to make it fit with what customers do want.

4 You may have started but be prepared to get additional help if you need it. It is still better to have a small piece of a big pie than a large piece of something tiny.

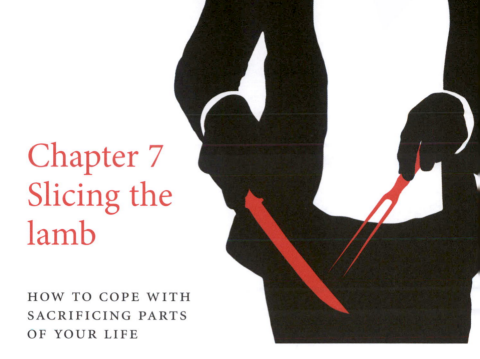

Chapter 7
Slicing the lamb

HOW TO COPE WITH
SACRIFICING PARTS
OF YOUR LIFE

'You have Guillain–Barré syndrome. You need to be in hospital tomorrow or you will end up on a respirator in a few days.'

'Christ, a respirator. What the hell is Guillain something syndrome?' I thought to myself, after this doctor gave me the good news.

'You need to rest. You are going to be in a hospital for at least six weeks. Maybe you can work again in February,' the cheery doctor continued.

But it was only early December. Christmas in hospital. Blimey I have got to stay in all that time. What about my business? How the hell can that rest? What about my people? I have to pay them next week.

Nick, my partner, told me to rest.

It's all bloody well him telling me to rest. He's putting in a fraction of the money I am. I am paying his salary, but no-one is paying mine. Jo, my wife, said that I needed to rest and must leave my PC behind. My shrink Billie said I needed to rest. Billie said 'There's an old expression in English – your nerves get frazzled – it means that your nerves literally tingle and don't function. That's what you have got. It's your mind telling your body to slow down. It's telling you that if you don't, it will! You must find a way to relax or it will get much more serious. Then your business won't count for much!'

'And what about the holiday we had booked in Paris for Christmas to celebrate my mother getting through her cancer? Fuck, I just can't walk. Well maybe I can?'

'No you can't. It will come back if you do too much too quickly,' the doctor reiterated.

Wikipedia told me that Guillain–Barré syndrome or GBS occurs most commonly as acute inflammatory demyelinating polyneuropathy. It is frequently severe and usually exhibits as an ascending paralysis noted by weakness in the legs that spreads to the upper limbs and the face along with complete loss of deep tendon reflexes. Death may occur if severe pulmonary complications and dysautonomia are present. That sounds serious! Maybe I do need to rest ...

Achieving a work–life balance is the most difficult part of living as an entrepreneur. So no bloody wonder that I had blown it. After all, I haven't had a proper work–life balance for over ten years. Is it any surprise that in this mad headlong rush to create my new business, I had sacrificed my health? Even Roland Rudd, the founder of Finsbury group, a global financial communications provider, who made his first Finsbury cheque even before he left his previous job at the FT, said 'my wife would say that I have sometimes sacrificed family life to create Finsbury.' And I reckoned Roland had suffered less than almost all the successful entrepreneurs that I knew.

> **Sacrifice is part of the bargain that you make as an entrepreneur.**

Sacrifice is part of the bargain that you make as an entrepreneur.

Mark de Wesselow said 'I regret sacrificing the care-free second half of my twenties. It was a great time to socialise but you needed disposable income. I was envious of some of the people who had steady jobs.'

Vaughan said of one of his sacrifices: 'I needed capital. Nobody thought it would work. I had to persuade my parents to borrow against all their assets. I would have destroyed the one thing that I had been brought up to protect, if it failed. My parents did not understand the project nor did they value it. My insistence caused a great deal of stress.'

As Lucy of Lovedean Granola said: 'Things have to give. It's a choice. I have no free time. I sacrifice sleep. I never watch a movie. I don't see my friends. It's hard for people to understand if they haven't been through the same thing.'

The trouble is you just can't switch off. Every

single entrepreneur I know says that it is a seven-days-a-week occupation. You can't just disappear for a week's holiday.

As I lay in my hospital bed, unable to sleep, my arms tingling from GBS, listening to the occasional screams of people on the neurology ward, I considered what I would do. How would this impact my decisions? Did this mean I wouldn't make it? And yet I didn't know what else I would do. I mean I would like to walk from London to Kabul but not now. I have an idea for an amazing theme park. I would like to own and restore a medieval castle. But I didn't want to do any of these until I had made this new business work. It was simply inconceivable. And yet my health was screwed. And the sad fact is that doctors don't really know what causes GBS. Mind you I knew that the stress over the past year had helped cause this. It was obvious. As any entrepreneur knows you are gambling – you are gambling money, health, family, love, self-respect, self-belief, friends and so many more things. It can hurt so much that it physically causes you pain.

Some sacrifices you don't notice until it's too late. The time you spend on your precious enterprise is time that you will never spend in the company of friends, family and loved ones. This doesn't just rob you. It robs them. It has a reciprocal effect on what they get out of life. They are on their own more. They don't have your attention. Do they need it? You don't ask. So you don't know. You work when the sun is

> The time you spend on your precious enterprise is time that you will never spend in the company of friends, family and loved ones.

out on the weekend and sometimes the endless pursuit does not always seem worth it.

And what about the others who really do need your help, which you too infrequently provide? My mother with cancer and the awful side effects of chemotherapy, stuck alone in Cognac in the middle of France at the age of 74. The times I failed to see her are the ones I will never get back.

I knew that I was sacrificing a conventional family life. My work came before everything – my wife, a normal life, my friendships, or the life that my father or mother had. I knew that I was sacrificing a certain amount of money – enough to buy a second house for example. But as long as you know what you will sacrifice then it helps. It means that although you won't like it, at least you will not regret it. You may hate the anguish, but you will understand the decisions you took. After all regret is a poisonous emotion. I was clear that I was prepared to sacrifice all of these things. Now of course you never know how far you will really go, but if you have really thought it through, then your gut tells you and you just have to go with that gut feeling.

But when you run into an unexpected sacrifice like ill-health, then you have to adapt and that, of course, is the other great saving grace of successful entrepreneurs – they can adapt. I knew that I had to find a way to get my good health back again. Whilst I said that I was prepared to accept sacrificing a number of things, ultimately I knew that I had to find a way to get balance or calm back into my life, or all my other sacrifices would be for nothing. And yet as the months go on and as a result of my illness, I find that the more stressed I get then the more the ends of my fingers and my toes get cold and tingly, literally like being frazzled. They act as a strange barometer for how stressed I am. All the time I am wondering whether I should push myself to get something done or whether I should pull back and rest for fear of ending up back in hospital. It's a strange live wire act trying to balance getting better health with getting my business going.

And as each new sacrifice comes, you question a little harder whether what you are doing is sensible. I had left my last job to start my business at exactly the same time that my mother got cancer in June 2008. By July 2009 I was mourning her untimely death. Strangely, when someone has died, you move faster than you ever did when they were alive – I was back in Cognac on the Monday, 24 hours after she was discovered by French firemen. Her poor fragile body had given up. We had talked of taking her to Italy in September when she finally finished her second bout of chemotherapy and I had spent months prevaricating about when to visit her – now I didn't prevaricate any longer. We cremated her on the Thursday. When it's all over you have to be comfortable with knowing that you have sacrificed something as important as looking after your mother in her hour of need.

So how do you deal with these sacrifices?

1 Learn to adapt. Learn to love the uncertainty, the surprises, the freedom, the wide open spaces of human possibilities, everything that so few people have. You have to love this incredible liberation from the straightjacket of corporate or public employment. You have to believe that there is no other way to move forward but to succeed. To succeed is to do what you love, creating something of your own that pays your way in life. How remarkable is that? If you learn to love that then in time it will create its own form of calm that relaxes you in the difficult times.

2 Talk about your sacrifices with others. Don't bottle them up. Stop occasionally and check that the sacrifices are worth it. Think about it.

3 Find a way to take your mind off the stress for a tiny amount of time each day. Find some way to do this. It's actually bloody hard to do, but it makes a real difference to your health and peace of mind.

4 See value in the 'journey' and not just the destination. If you enjoy the ups and downs of the process then you will find it easier to cope with the inevitable sacrifices.

5 Find comfort in striving after your own goals in life. If this is important to you then you can take comfort in knowing that you are doing something that matters, whatever the sacrifice.

Chapter 8 Friends, allies and mentors

HOW TO SEEK HELP FROM PEOPLE AROUND YOU

'The Chris I once knew probably has all the angles figured out, plus any relevant curves, tangents and percentages.'

When I read that line at the end of Melanie's email, I almost cried.

Melanie worked for me eight years ago. She is an incredibly smart Oxford graduate, with a wealth of knowledge across a range of disciplines from writing to research and web development to event management. Yet here now on an email, eight years after we last spoke to each other, was

just an amazing vote of confidence. It was a vote of confidence in my ability and my apparent invincibility, at a time when actually such votes of confidence were few and far between. It was priceless to me.

It was all the more poignant because, in truth, I didn't have all the answers figured out. In fact when Melanie found our site, it was totally serendipitous, as she knew much more about social media than I did. I was hunting for people who could help and she just popped up. Wow. That's the crazy thing about being an entrepreneur: coincidences seem to happen every day. It doesn't seem to work like that in corporate life or in a standard 9–5 existence. People just do what they do and go home.

> You need people to comment on what you are doing, to praise, to reassure, to challenge and even to criticise.

Why do you need people? Because we all run into problems. Entrepreneurs run into them every day and often have no bloody idea how to resolve them. You have to ask for help to solve them. You have to learn to ask for help about lots of things on a daily basis. As they say you often don't have more than 50% of the available information to take a decision or solve a problem. And yet take decisions is what you need to do. So you need to use friends and allies whenever and wherever you can. As an entrepreneur you are a hunter, gathering, striking out and cunningly seeking your goal. Some people can do it on their own but most can't. And so you need people to comment on what you are doing, to praise, to reassure, to challenge and even to criticise. You need it all.

As Peter Christiansen said, 'I have tried to rely on too few people. I underestimated the power of a network.'

While William Reeve of LOVEFiLM said 'I rely on my network of people. Most of the £2m (I raised for LOVEFiLM) came from connections of mine.'

And this is the amazing thing with humanity, the capacity of people to surprise one with their generosity and support. If you are open to it you get it. People will help you in all sorts of ways. And in their emotional support are tiny signs of belief, belief that you can do it, that you can overcome things.

I have found that there are seven types of people you encounter as an entrepreneur and not all of them are helpful! The seven types are rejectors, doubters, enquirers, allies, advocates, friends and mentors. You have to know how to deal with them all. You also have to recognise that some people will be in more than one camp!

Rejectors think you will fail. They are bad news. They sap your natural enthusiasm and energy. When you encounter them, move away. They don't help.

Doubters are different. They can be anyone from a VC who is unconvinced, to a friend who thinks you are mad to do this. They tend not to bother to see your latent strengths. These people are useful. See them as the enemy, the competition. Focus on proving them wrong. As Sun Tzu said in *The Art of War*, opportunities come from openings in the environment caused by relative weaknesses in your enemy within a given area. Doubters help you to see your weaknesses but also help highlight the assumptions in the current market. Unknowingly they help you to exploit these assumptions.

Bruce Dodworth was a doubter. Bruce is a classically trained PR man, who now works for himself and advises many large corporates on their communications and PR strategy. Like many good PR people he has an unerring sense of how the media will view something and how you can try to shape your message accordingly. I hired Bruce to do our PR when I was helping Icomera, the world's first company to put wireless Internet access on trains, with their marketing.

Now, I was asking for his advice on our PR strategy, just as a friend and someone who I had once worked with. And he gave it, not just once but several times over several months without charging me a penny. He started out as a sceptic, a doubter, and he just didn't get the idea. But over time as we discussed it and as he gave advice, he started to get it. He was a massive help to us at a time when we were too close to our own service to see the wood from the trees. People don't need to but they do it. You can get advice from doubters and it can be very helpful, because if you convince them then you are half way to success. So plunder your contacts when you need to!

Enquirers are all about you. They are curious

about what you are doing. They don't reveal themselves as being either positive or negative. They just want to know more and in some cases they want to know if there is a useful angle for themselves. They won't necessarily tell you what they have concluded but sometimes they do. These people are worth engaging with. They could be allies or partners or they could just give you a glimpse of how different people and companies are reacting to your business. This is often helpful. Frequently you find enquirers in large companies who are interested in smaller start-ups. It's easy to be paranoid about these guys and whether they will steal your ideas. In fact I find they provide useful perspectives. I have gone to see the CEOs of FTSE 100 companies as well as people looking to start businesses in the same space. And one in five times something valuable results from it. That's a useful ratio!

Allies are quietly positive. They may not help you in all sorts of overt ways and yet they provide a calm supportive barrier for you against the less supportive. Look after them. Praise them. When they want a favour give it to them. Eric is a supporter and an ally. He has his own business, the Third Space, which I think is probably the best gym in the world. He said our business idea was a no brainer and made sense to them. He has continued to support it.

Advocates have ceaseless belief in you. They praise you and see all the plus points and many fewer negatives. They need to be part of your

> Allies are quietly positive. Look after them. Praise them. When they want a favour give it to them.

ongoing crusade. They can help you excite others. Jo, my wife, is an advocate amongst other things! She has provided incredible support. She has listened to my endless rantings about the business. It's not just once a day but 20 times a day. She listens and advises and smiles. She also pushes me to see the positives and to express the success stories. Without her support life would have been twice as difficult. You need advocates all the time.

Victoria Baillieu of Pay Check said they found an advocate: 'We had a "godfather" – an insolvency accountant. He would review our accounts and have meetings with us. He would say: "I suppose I have to take you to dinner because you can't afford the water!" He would send us masses of business. He was very influential for us. He would give us work and introduce us to people.'

> Friends are just there for you. They don't give up on you and help whenever they can.

Friends are just there for you. They don't give up on you and help whenever they can. You will take these people for granted, but in time you will realise that and hopefully repay it. Jonathan and Hacer used to work for me years ago. They are both very smart and straight. They have provided countless amounts of support, giving advice and constructive criticism. Truly it's awe inspiring. It's humbling. As Mark de Wesselow said of his future wife, Katherine, 'Most girls would not have stuck with me. I didn't have a lot of time, a lot of money or a lot of commitment. It was tough.'

Finally there are mentors. Mentors are guides.

They give you advice, based on real and practical experience. Sometimes they have been in your shoes and sometimes they just have the expertise to understand what it is like and what the choices are. They don't judge you or chastise you. It's your business after all and not theirs. They are just trying to help as an objective and friendly voice in business. Whether they fully believe or not they support you. They are really helpful but hard to find. Seek them out.

And don't be afraid of ignoring their advice either, as Ingrid Murray said: 'I found it difficult to ask other's opinion because I felt duty bound to act on it if I did ask. I had to learn that you can be confident to ask and it didn't oblige you to follow it up.'

I have had mentors in the past. Frequently I have ignored their advice, but more often than not they have been right and I have been wrong. It is humbling when you realise this! In fact I would recommend that anyone starting a business finds a mentor *before* they start.

I didn't have a mentor when we started You Wish and I wish I had. It was an oversight. They might have helped me see some of my mistakes earlier.

Strangely in many workplaces asking for help is not encouraged. But when you are on your own, it's not begging. It's more like busking! You are performing. You are the source of inspiration to many as you are doing something different. You have to capture that and use it. Some people say what you are doing is brilliant; others say it's a good idea but … and others still say very little. Their points of view are all interesting and there is value in almost all of them. And when someone asks you how your empire is developing, you smile and say 'Brilliantly!'

And that is really what it is all about – being able to smile and see the positives in what you are doing and let people around you into your life. People you don't expect give you support. People you have just met and people you have known for years.

Five critical things that may help you leverage your friends and allies.

1 See the hand of friendship and support anywhere and everywhere. Ask people about what they are doing. Talk to people about what you are doing. Talk to people who you might not normally. Look for chance encounters, for new people, for new opportunities. You never know what value can be created until you look laterally at it. New people help you to do that. They take you out of your comfort zone and subject you to new challenges. Who knows what words of wisdom or connections you will then make?

2 Do a good deed for others. Actively seek to help others out. Join networks of similar people and become a positive contributor. If you are open to helping others, they will help you. Make allies of people everywhere you go, and then you can call upon their help, when you need it.

3 Don't be scared of getting found out for not having all the answers. You won't have them all. Be transparent and benefit from your candour.

4 Flirt, charm and use every trick in the book and tool in your armoury to engage with people.

5 Look back at your career to date and identify the people who you respect and still see. They are most likely to be people who have a little more experience than you and who always have something valuable to say about what you are doing. Approach one of them and see if they can be a mentor as you embark on your new business.

HOW DO YOU TELL THE GOOD GUYS FROM THE BAD?

1. Will they instinctively offer you help or do you have to ask for it?
2. Are they interested in you personally or some other agenda?
3. Have they helped others before – what is their reputation like?
4. Would you be happy to help them, just because you like or respect them?

Chapter 9 When jealousy is a good thing

HOW TO USE YOUR FEELINGS OF JEALOUSY PRODUCTIVELY

'They looked at what you were doing and thought they had a much better business model.'

When Andy said that, I was really pissed off. Andy was my old boss in advertising and now an angel investor. He always puts it simple and straight!

But the trouble is the truth hurt.

I actually thought this competitor to You Wish had a better business model too! They were an online service that also turned the traditional selling model on its head. The critical difference between us was that they had a very simple and very effective route to market, having partnered with a large automotive magazine and the biggest property website and both of these drove large amounts of traffic to their website for potentially high value transactions. They also had a former senior figure in online search on their board and that added real insight.

The fact that Andy went on to say that 'I told him that I thought you were both doing different things, with different strategies' was surprisingly little consolation.

In fact I think we are trying to do different things, but it still niggled at me. It really threw me for a few hours.

And that's the problem with jealousy: it is insidious. It's poisonous. It just chips and chips at your confidence.

One day you can think you're ahead of your competition and the next, it's a real shock to see someone doing better than you, who you never knew existed. But you always have to remember that competition is a good thing and indeed an essential thing. If you don't have any competition then you don't have a market. And without a market, you don't have a business.

> If you don't have any competition then you don't have a market. And without a market, you don't have a business.

Every now and then you see a competitor go bust and you have a brief moment of satisfaction. I remember one of our (syzygy) original competitors in the Internet space, a web agency called Webmedia. They were the best known of the early web agencies in the mid 1990s. One day they just imploded having run out of cash. We felt great. We were now ready to take over the mantle of leading UK web agency. And yet within another 12 months another 20 agencies had burst on to the scene and we were competing with them instead!

I think jealousy comes in different forms – three different flavours, plain vanilla, rocky road and cherry, to be more precise!

Firstly, plain vanilla jealousy. You can just be jealous of people who are making a lot of money, while you're not. It always tends to be the same villains! They are generally bankers. They just make more money than anyone else. It seems unfair and it makes me jealous when I think how much they do make, but actually I don't want to be a banker, so who cares? And then of course you have the accountants and lawyers, who are like perennials. They flower every year without fail! They are people you can't live without and get paid a lot at the same time.

Secondly, rocky road. There are people who are true competitors in your space. They are close by. And sometimes they are just that bit further ahead than you. They aren't necessarily making any more money or doing that much better, but even a little better can feel agonising. They might win a bigger contract than you. They might introduce something to the market that is very innovative and PR-worthy. Or they might expand to another country or sector before you do.

Thirdly, there's cherry flavour. You have to accept that there are people who are entrepreneurs in another space, who are doing well, doing better than you. They are making money and receiving plaudits for their activities.

That just pisses you off because you curse yourself for not having come up with that idea instead of your own!

At different times they can all irritate you and sometimes they can make you spitting mad. And as society tries to teach you this is not a helpful emotion.

But is jealousy actually such a bad thing? Sometimes as an entrepreneur jealousy can be a powerful weapon that can help you achieve more.

As Jeffrey O'Rourke says: 'Within the management team, it's like a court of your peers. People are trying to impress each other. It's pride. Intellectually it's a motivator. I remember one Christmas reading about Google, thinking that I could have done that. It's interesting to watch contemporaries that suddenly rise above us. Why him? Why her? They aren't brighter or better.'

It can also inspire you as Nick Wheeler of Charles Tyrwhitt said: 'Boden has a fantastic business. They have worked out what they are about. I admire them. I look at people like Paul Smith and they inspire me. He has built a great business. I am a tortoise and he is a tortoise. I want to build a great business and it is inspirational to see what they have done. I would have loved to have started Carphone Warehouse. I try to channel it positively.'

It forces you to rework your thinking, to challenge the real essence of your business and to look for better solutions. Ultimately what

> Sometimes as an entrepreneur jealousy can be a powerful weapon that can help you achieve more.

jealousy should do is make you identify how to leapfrog your competition. It should help you see how to turn the tables on them and outplay them. It can do this because if they think they have a better model, then they can become lazy and accept traditional assumptions. You on the other hand have to fight dirty. You have to use every trick in the book, every plan that you can find in any industry that allows you to cut up rough.

So don't let jealousy hinder your plans. Leverage the energy it brings to create a positive effect. Here are some specific ways to use jealousy positively:

1 Don't focus on the competition all the time. It causes too much negativity. Make yourself analyse them at a set time each week or month and use that time constructively. But when you are not doing that, then just focus on your own business.

2 Deconstruct their model and try to define exactly which elements are better and why. Take each element in turn, whether it is the product, or the business model, or the route to market or the partnerships and think about what you could do for each one that is better than this. What in each case is an improvement for your customer? How can you leapfrog each element and so devise something unassailably better? And don't feel any guilt about copying the little things while you look to outflank them on the bigger ones.

3 Remember that you are trying to be better or different doing your own thing, not slavishly copying them. So follow your own path and don't be afraid to be different.

4 Reflect on your positives. They do exist. You have your own strengths. You just need to understand them and use them. You can both succeed. There is never a proper functioning market with only one player in it.

5 Consider whether what your competition is doing suggests that you have some gaps in your skillbase, which you need to fill. Are you blindsided by anything?

6 Talk about your competitive fears and worries. Don't bottle them up. Get other people to give you a view. Not only will this put things in perspective, but it will also give you an honest view of where you stand.

HOW DO YOU FLIRT SUCCESSFULLY IN BUSINESS?

1. Smile. Most people wander around looking miserable. Smiling at people makes you likeable – that's half the battle.
2. Be interested. Don't feign interest. Be genuinely interested. Care about what is going on in other people's lives. How was their evening? Are they OK?
3. Be kind. Go the extra mile for someone.
4. Be bold. Do something unexpected. Stand for something. Make yourself different. Make yourself someone people want to get to know.

Chapter 10
Pals or partners

'I'm fed up with you telling me what the fuck to do. Just get off my case. The business is going to be fine,' I yelled at my business partner.

You mess it up in business for the same reasons that you mess it up at home. Either somebody gets bored and starts screwing around, or both sides can only focus on their respective weaknesses and the business does not develop or the relationship ends up becoming unequal. Ultimately passions can run high and spoil the party. In the end you can't stand being in the same room as your partner. I have been there. I can remember just wanting to punch the guy's lights out.

There is no surprise in this.

The business relationship is incredibly intimate. It's about hopes, dreams and fortunes and frequently disasters when it goes wrong.

Hell, one spends more time with one's business partner than with your own husband, wife, girlfriend or boyfriend. The business relationship is incredibly intimate. It's about hopes, dreams and fortunes and frequently disasters when it goes wrong. It brings amazing highs and lows.

If you have early success and big dreams, it tends to cement relationships and to bring you together.

I can remember travelling to New York in early 1997 with my business partner John. We had won a few big clients together including Mars and Cartoon Network and were feeling invincible. We were going to take the New York Internet market by storm and yet we were only generating a few hundred thousand pounds in revenues. Nothing could stop us. We were testosterone-heavy and full of British charm. We didn't conquer the USA but we did do Europe, floating the business in 2000 on the German Stock Exchange for €240m.

But there are a number of warning signs that indicate that the relationship may be going sour, sooner than you realise:

- You are not being fair and honest with each other, either in terms of your respective workload and commitment or in terms of money.
- You've stopped supporting each other publicly and are moaning about each other at every opportunity.

- There's an unspoken truth: you just don't trust each other any longer.

When these warning signs start appearing you know you need to stop and give the relationship some proper consideration, because soon you'll stop talking. By this point you argue so much when you do talk, that it is easier not to talk. When this happens you have to make sorting this out the number-one priority. You have to take time out to resolve it. This could be time out together or time out on your own. Sometimes it gets sufficiently bad that you need external help to mediate. Certainly in the early days of a start-up when ideas are still germinating, it is possible to find that different people want to go in different directions. This is unfortunately natural and sometimes you just have to let things split. But unless you sit round the table and talk about where you want to go and what's working and what's not, it won't work. Then it'll just explode.

I remember John and I used to talk outside of syzygy's offices because we had started arguing so much and we didn't want the others to see it. In fact the pressure valve got taken off because John started another business and I stayed focused on syzygy.

We've all seen companies where the founders have started to criticise each other in public. It has a devastatingly negative impact on other people. If it appears that you can't work together then why should anyone else think that it is OK to work with your company? If this happens get some external help. Get a chairman to mediate. Find a solution that deals with it. Ultimately if you can't find a solution, then it may be better for one of the founders to leave and let the business keep going positively. This sounds terrible, but often it is in everyone's best interests if some value continues to be built in the start-up rather than it all implodes and no-one gets anything!

It pays to make an effort on both sides. As Matt Norton of Sentry Wireless says about his business partner: 'We have very good communication. We are very clear that it is not personal. It's not a criticism of the individual. We both make an effort to be considerate of the other person. We are very collaborative. We rarely make decisions without offering people a chance to voice their opinion.'

It also pays to be realistic. As Jeffrey O'Rourke said: 'People are good at different things. Use their strengths and accept their weaknesses. Try to improve the latter.'

Sometimes women have a better attitude to this than men, as Victoria Baillieu of Pay Check said of her relationship with her business partner, Sophie: 'We both have the view that not everything can be a battlefield. If I feel very strongly about something then Sophie will probably go with it, and vice versa. We understand together and individually what we have to do.' This pragmatism is invaluable in a start-up.

And give each other space as Greg Hadfield of Soccernet said about his son Tom: 'There were times when Tom just wanted me to be Dad and not pitching him another idea. But I know a lot of stuff and this was interesting to him. Whilst we were putting up football scores, we would be talking about the big issues of mankind. There was real camaraderie, but there were times when I was crowding him!'

Assuming that you're still talking, the other key requirement is to create some natural rhythm in the relationship. In almost all business relationships, rituals play an important role in achieving this. They provide a strange sense of comfort at an uncomfortable time. Frequently these rituals revolve around meeting places and eating and drinking. Before Nick, my business partner, and I began, we used to meet in what we thought was the most expensive meeting room in London – the Athenaeum Hotel on Piccadilly where we ate the cheapest thing on the menu, 'Piccadilly porkers' (sausages to you and me!), but at least you didn't have to pay to sit there all day. To compensate we would take large numbers of smart magazines from the lounge and free jelly babies from reception. For a while there was a certain waitress there, Laura, with whom we would all flirt. Every comment and titter brought us together. Tiny pleasures at a time of great stress. Once the business was started we would go to Frank's café and talk about global domination over eggs, sausages and chips! It doesn't really matter where it is as

> The other key requirement is to create some natural rhythm in the relationship.

long as there is some subconscious stability in behaviour.

Of course these relationships require laughter and war stories. It's why there is an emerging industry in creating company myths that drive the workforce forward together. But actually these relationships often require serious mutual support. People are under a lot of strain and so you often need to have a drink together to chill out and let off steam. On these occasions, it's amazing how easy it is to swap stories about all sorts of personal issues with people you may not have known for long. This could be marital or relationship problems. It can be money problems. And so as the candle burns you learn a remarkable amount about your fellow business partners in a very short space of time. Often this is late into the evening when your guard is down. It doesn't actually matter if it helps you all gel together. That's the key to success.

But equally you have to remember that this is still business.

Sometimes you just need to keep some distance. Matthew Page, manager of Feeder, stressed how this was actually critical to his success: 'We have done it all together. We've been smashed in some brothel in Tokyo. I had a very emotional evening there with one of the band. He saw me as a broken man. We've done it all. But the reason we have kept together is because I have kept a little aloof. I have focused on the business above everything.'

But what if it isn't just business, what if your

> People are under a lot of strain and so you often need to have a drink together to chill out and let off steam.

partner is your husband, as it was for Janie
Brown of Jane Brown Shoes? Janie started out
on her own in 1997 and quickly attracted the
attention of luxury store Bergdorf Goodman,
which opened up the shoe world for her and led
to her husband, Paul, joining her in the business
a couple of years later.

Janie says: 'I loved the idea of working with
Paul. It all felt very nice and organic. The kids
growing up, us all together, all going to trade
fairs. I trusted him completely. It was delightful.
But the business changed as we started to employ
people and I began relinquishing responsibilities
to others. I took on a more one-dimensional role
as the designer. We thought it worked because
we were so wrapped up in it, schools, training
staff, looking after children, trade fairs at half
term. We were comforting each other, but we
weren't growing the business in a way teams
grow businesses.'

Also, there's often a power struggle. Janie went
on to explain: 'Having done it myself and seen
a lot of success, I baulked when Paul suggested
something I didn't believe in, I'd learnt to trust
my instincts, choosing factories and people to
work with. To have my husband override my gut
instinct was very difficult, so I started to distrust
his gut instinct. It hurts men more than women
realise. I was sometimes making it quite difficult
for him to do his job. If he hadn't been my
husband I would still have disagreed with him,
but it wouldn't have felt as personal.

With a business partner, you naturally become

exacting and critical, but to become exacting and critical of your husband is not a good thing. A business partner has to perform. But if your business partner performs, but differently to how you expect and he is your husband, what do you do? You can hurt each other. And who is to say I was right?'

Well, if you're family then it's sensible to see this earlier rather than later! It's better to keep the marriage going and maybe the business, rather than kill them both. Be prepared to take the hard decision. And if you are going to do both at the same time, then find a way to leave the 'office' behind. As Jo Fairley of Green & Black's says: 'Craig [Jo's husband and business partner] and I depended on each other. Most of my friends are not in business. You can't expect them to understand. But we tried to quarantine our anxiety for one hour every evening. We talked about all the issues and then we were banned from discussing it for the rest of the evening. It helped to compartmentalise things.'

And similarly, if you're not family, and the trust goes because one party starts to do other things or even starts another business, well then one side has probably broken their side of the bargain. You have to deliver to each other. If you can't, then maybe it's time to split.

So how do you make it work? There are some basics that you need to get right:

1 Honour your commitments. Partners have to learn their strengths and weaknesses and

give and take. I paid Nick to write up a detailed commercial proposition that would form the precursor to the business plan. I felt he did a mediocre job. He agreed it was not perfect and that I did not have to pay him. But I felt that I needed to honour my commitment to him if we were to trust each other going forward. I had not specified the work well enough and so was partially to blame. If you can't honour your commitment, then come clean and tell your business partner about it. Don't wait for it to blow up in your faces. And then try to find an alternative solution.

2 Know and understand how your business partners operate. John Bates, Adjunct Professor of Entrepreneurship, London Business School and entrepreneur says: 'Practice is the most important part of making it work with your fellow entrepreneurs. You have to know how they operate. It is not like an employment relationship. It is based on trust. It is much more intuitive.'

3 Talk. And then talk some more. You have to communicate. You have to say when you feel you have been let down. You have to give praise when it is due. You have to listen even if you don't agree. If you don't give good direction then people get lost. If you're the boss then make sure your people know what is expected of them. The reason the army has such precise command structures and rules is because they will be hopelessly ineffective if people get lost or don't know what to do.

4 Go mad occasionally. Have fun. Get pissed. When you try to start a business, you have to have some fun in what is a very stressful situation.

5 Get external mediation if it's not working. Find someone independent and pay them to sit you down and get you to talk to each other and work through the problems.

6 Respect your partner's need for space. If they need time out with their family or whatever, then let it be. If you cramp each other too much, it will explode.

Part 3
In the danger zone

WHEN YOU'RE FULLY COMMITTED EMOTIONALLY AND MATERIALLY, AND HAVE BEEN WORKING ON THE BUSINESS FOR A WHILE, IT STARTS TO GET HARDER, BEFORE IT GETS EASIER.

You are making progress, but it's not as fast as you need. There are some positive early signs but you will have had a couple of setbacks. You need to think differently about things to see if you can get some real momentum going. You need the right mindset now as this is the hardest part – it's the grind:

- Maybe you need to challenge your own assumptions a bit more. Could you make more progress if you dropped that view of your business? How do you shift your mindset and adapt as you really experience the market? Many of the great entrepreneurs are like boxers – really good at moving faster than others and seeing new ways to do things and new opportunities. You need to be like them.

- It's a nuisance but you need to work with a bunch of expensive lawyers and accountants and other advisers to get things done. How do you make this work?

- How do you deal with all the uncertainty? Most humans love certainty and stability. You need to know how to manage when there isn't much of that around.

- You have to make decisions all the time, but how do you get them right? Maybe you need to trust your instincts a bit more than you did. You need to feel the right way.

- How do you keep everyone else going? How do you keep your team motivated? How do you keep the dream alive if there's lots of disappointment around?

- How do you cope with rejection? How do you deal with the crushing blows of disinterest and failure that seem to rain down on you? And they can do.

Now is not the time to lose heart. No, now is the time to show your mettle. And the first step is to be flexible in your thinking, to act quicker than others because you are more open-minded to the possibilities.

Chapter 11
Challenging your own assumptions

HOW TO GET GOOD AT CHALLENGING YOUR OWN BELIEFS

'Why don't you raise money in Qatar? It's a huge opportunity. They have lots of money and are looking to invest in the industries of the future, and I can put you in touch with the right people.' My energetic 60-year-old Australian aunt, Georgie, asked me this over dinner. She is very well connected and is raising money herself, although for rather larger sums than me for the mining industry!

And there I was thinking that I was about to tie up a deal with a UK angel investment network and try to raise the money here in London. Mind you I thought that the network charges were exorbitantly high for no guarantee. It raised an interesting opportunity and, in truth, Georgie wasn't the first person to suggest that I try to raise money in the Middle East. But could I do all of these things at once? It opened up another avenue and new avenues are always intriguing to the entrepreneur. It was another way forward; a way out of the current predicament. But if I turned down the UK route now then I might have to wait until September to go again and it was only the beginning of June and I had nearly run out of money. I couldn't do it. Well I don't think I could, not now anyway.

The day before, the business we were hoping to cement as our first channel partner came back with a completely different proposition. We had suggested a business-to-business solution with them paying us a licence fee up front – to help cash flows – and then doing a revenue share of 20%. Now they had come back with a counter offer, proposing a consumer service with a joint venture split 50–50 and no up-front monies. We had always assumed that we could do revenue shares only giving away a small percentage, but now we had the opportunity to sell our first one and the deal needed to be 50–50. The upside that they proposed was that we also partnered with a very large consumer brand, who would then do the marketing under their brand. But, if we went this way it meant accepting that we might have to do several sector-specific third-party deals and then could we really compete with our own cross-sector consumer service? This was potentially a fundamentally different strategy.

And maybe it was an indication of how our first strategy needed to change. If we did the deal, it would be our first deal. Hell, we would be able to raise our first external funding. It would mean all that hard work had finally paid off. So it was a case of having a big piece of a small pie or a small piece of a big pie! Surely having part of the bigger pie was better than no pie at all!

One of the most emotionally draining things about being an entrepreneur is that you need to be alive to your assumptions changing all the time. At the very least you need to change or adapt them all the time. You can't stand still. You need to be receptive to new suggestions and yet stay true to your objectives. Most humans find this level of mental change and agility difficult to bear. After all it is unsettling. Indeed most big companies teach people to develop plans and then to execute them exactly as they stand and to the best of their abilities, but actually as an entrepreneur with a start-up, you need to do the reverse. You need to have an end goal but be very prepared to change the plan a number of times along the way.

It also helps to have a business partner. As Matt Norton of Sentry Wireless said: 'Having a partner is key: you can look each other in the eye and say "That is bollocks, you're dreaming!" And, equally, when you hit on something that you believe is good, you know it is good because you *both* can see it.'

In fact, being a successful entrepreneur often means taking a very different stance on an

> You can't stand still. You need to be receptive to new suggestions and yet stay true to your objectives.

issue. It means deliberately breaking a set of norms or established wisdom. Many successful new companies do just that. They change the dynamics of a market or turn the business model on its head. In other words, they change the way their company in a given industry creates value. Look at how Zara transformed the fashion industry by bringing catwalk fashion to the high street at speed and cheaply, or how Zopa and now Wonga are trying to change the banking world with peer-to-peer lending models. Consider how Nespresso challenged the traditional model of selling coffee through retailers by going direct to the consumer in their home and makes 32 pence for every cup you drink. It's the change in the model or how you pay that signals to people that it is a different proposition.

Ink started life in the heady days of 2000 when the first dotcom boom was coming to an end. We raised over £10m in funding to take classic offline content and repurpose it and sell it online. Yet after nearly running out of money in 2003, we transformed what we did and by 2008 the company was doing something completely different and had become the world's largest contract publisher of in-flight magazines. Few start-up companies end up in the same place as they started, because in spite of up-front market research and planning, finding the sweet spot is incredibly hard to pinpoint in advance.

Surviving the early stages of a start-up is often about learning how to adapt fast to

Surviving the early stages of a start-up is often about learning how to adapt fast to change.

change. Looking again at early assumptions and reformulating them can become liberating. It allows you to move quicker than others around you. You don't have to deal with the baggage of years of entrenched behaviour or traditions or established assumptions about your market.

As John Bates, of London Business School says: 'The only thing we can guarantee is that your business plan is wrong and that you will need more money. The real issue is how quickly do you adapt to reality? Changing reality to meet your plan is probably going to fail! You need to challenge your assumptions daily, weekly and all the time while at the same time pretending that you know where you are going!'

This subject is comprehensively covered in a book by John Mullins and Randy Komisar called *Getting to Plan B*. This book tackles this key entrepreneurial issue – the fact that so many new start-ups are founded on false assumptions – and that the best entrepreneurs quickly wake up to this problem and adapt their plans. The authors reference a research statistic that shows that only one in 58 new product ideas works. They stress the importance of redoing the business plan every time your carefully tracked evidence suggests that the business model won't work until you get there. That is what I was starting to do with You Wish Plan A!

It's about having the right mindset as Ingrid Murray said: 'Being a learner is an important part and you need to be quite flexible. One day I will be knee deep in mud talking to a pig farmer. The next day I am in the bank. You need a willingness to give things a go and to listen to people.'

We researched our ideas for You Wish extensively before we started and developed a number of carefully constructed and market-tested assumptions, but how wrong we were. We started with the belief that You Wish needed to work across several need areas or sectors nationally. Then we adapted our thinking to focus just on health, fitness and beauty, but people often ignored what we proposed and so we changed our approach again to target services rather than products. And now we are refocusing on a strategy of targeting local communities where you can recruit across all sectors within a smaller region. We started out thinking that our service was just about people engaging with companies and that peer-to-peer community was unimportant but now have concluded that the community is also critical to success. So many assumptions that we started with have proved to be wrong and have needed changing – in some cases fundamentally. Or did we just never resolve the original partnership question – the need to get a large partner to drive traffic to us cost effectively?

Changing assumptions can drive you mad or you can learn to enjoy it. I have begun to find it quite satisfying. When people actually tell you that your new strategy is a real improvement, then you can justifiably feel really good about the change. You just have to be able to let go of the past. You have to learn not to reproach yourself for decisions that you took a while ago. They can't change, but you can change going forward …

So how do you get good at this? There are a few tricks to this:

1 Be crystal clear about your vision and then focus on the execution. You can't re-examine them both all the time. You should continually re-examine how you want to get there, but only occasionally relook at the vision or you will just go round in circles.

2 Separate out what's important, what's urgent and what sounds exciting. They are all different. Focus on the key drivers towards what is important and strategic and not what's urgent or sexy.

3 Focus on how you create value – how a customer is going to be better off because of what you do.

4 Chew on problems that people raise. Don't just ignore them and hope that they go away. They won't, particularly if lots of people raise them. From the word go, smart people have said to me that You Wish would only work with channel partners. I have always accepted that this would be the case, but have not found it easy to find the right partners. But I have always been looking for them. I never forgot that challenge.

I now have channel partners after a long search. You just have to keep re-examining the problem and different ways to solve it.

5 Embrace finding new solutions, new ways of doing things. Enjoy reading and listening to other ways of cracking problems. And, like a magpie, be prepared to steal good ideas wherever you see them. This is war and you need all the supplies and reinforcements you can get.

Chapter 12 Loving the middleman

HOW TO MAKE THE MOST OF THE NECESSARY INTERMEDIARIES

'I began to hate the bureaucrats who made our business difficult to work. People who made it difficult without trying to understand what we were doing; parking wardens, councillors, suppliers, employees who would steal from you, the list goes on. The anger gives you determination.'

Vaughan said this to me some five years after he started the Frontline Club.

I could relate to all of this. I found it so easy to get pissed off and rant against any intermediary I encountered who just appeared to be making a fast buck at my expense. I had just spoken to my accountants the day before and had explained that I wanted a quote for some advice on some tax and investment issues. I had explicitly said I needed a quote before I incurred any costs, so why had the tax manager sent me an email two days later giving me a quote but saying that I had already incurred a charge for my earlier conversation? It was unbelievable. I mean genuinely unbelievable. How could they do that? It made me speechless.

So who are these people that you will need to work with and depend on for your livelihood? Well it will probably include a smattering of some of these: accountants, lawyers, tax advisers, the Inland Revenue, manufacturers, distributors, council staff, health and safety and maybe a trade union or two.

The truth is you can either resent them or work out how to make the most of them. After all, ranting at them may make you feel marginally better for a nanosecond, but it won't actually change your situation. Whether you like it or not, you are going to have to work with them and you might as well get comfortable with this fact. You need lawyers to draw up contracts, you need accountants to do your accounts, you need payroll to organise your payroll and the Inland Revenue needs you to submit a bunch of forms on a regular basis.

The good news is that many intermediaries recognise that it is expensive to use them and are now being creative in how they help entrepreneurs.

There is an unwritten law that I follow which is that if you are going to give someone some business, then they will give you a bit of help up front for free. Use this rule to help you out. Make sure that any form of professional adviser or intermediary does something of value for you before you hire them. It's a good old fashioned quid pro quo.

You need to learn that some middlemen can be unexpectedly helpful and generous with their time.

In fact, if you are going to be successful, you need to learn that some middlemen can be unexpectedly helpful and generous with their time. A lawyer may give you some free help on an employment contract or an accountant may help you on an issue to do with shares.

And sometimes it's just a case of treating them nicely. I can remember taking one of the Inland Revenue managers out to lunch to help lubricate the wheels when they discovered that we had not been paying the full tax on our company expenses for several years. It took a very good bottle of wine to help get over it!

They can also be good fun when called upon. They like a good time as much as anyone. When we were doing our syzygy IPO roadshow across Europe, we were escorted very ably by HSBC executives. They would wine and dine us all the hours that we weren't presenting to potential investors. And the great thing was they had to stay for as long as you stayed out. Yes you were paying for it but hell I was sure going to enjoy it. So in Amsterdam, Dusseldorf, Zurich, Paris and even Glasgow we did our best to oblige! I remember emerging from one Dusseldorf bar at 6am to find an HSBC exec waiting to pay the bill and escort me back to my hotel in a waiting taxi. Now that's service.

Sometimes the unexpected happens and you have to try to turn it to your advantage, as Lucy of Lovedean Granola said: 'When my manufacturer said we're going nut free, I thought my world had collapsed. I had been given two months' notice. I had to find another manufacturer. So now I have a bakery and am very happy. It's like my own kitchen. I have much more control and so I am very happy.'

And then every now and again you find an intermediary who works purely on a performance basis. They deliver genuine high-quality work and service that is only rewarded when value is created. Well, that is amazing.

So how do you deal with intermediaries?

Here are a few critical things to remember:

1 Don't be jealous of their well-paid and safe lifestyle. You're the exciting one. Imagine that they want a piece of your excitement.

2 Understand them like you would a customer. Be clear on what their needs and objectives are. Then consider how and if you fit with these.

3 Test out whether they are really interested in what you are doing before you commit. If they won't give anything up front then avoid them.

4 Make sure you extract maximum value for your money, but agree it all in advance.

5 Spend time networking to find the good guys who are prepared to help out and invest in new start-ups on the basis that many will work and deliver them fees over the long run.

6 Always double and triple check that you are clear about what they want before you start. It's bloody obvious, but do read the terms and conditions. You find all sorts of things in there that you won't know about.

Chapter 13 Not knowing

COPING WITH UNCERTAINTY

'Chris, in three months' time my family and I are out on the street if we haven't raised the money. I can't let that happen. I have already extended our mortgage.' It was March and Nick, my business partner, was getting edgier every day. Money was running short. I had made the decision to hold off going for funding because we weren't ready. Now we were, but we're unlikely to get it in time. By June Nick only had one month left and I had three!

This scares the life out of you. Twenty-four hours a day you worry, you wonder, you stress. It's bloody hard never knowing what will happen and what the right answer is to anything. In most established industries, there are only a few strategies or

The great entrepreneur exploits the lack of knowledge to keep ahead of the game.

rules of the game and it is merely a question of how you move around the board. In new or developing industries there is much less certainty and knowledge. It's always a case of trying to extend the range of moves you have on the chess board, rather than let the options evaporate around you.

The great entrepreneur exploits the lack of knowledge to keep ahead of the game, but for most mortals the uncertainty is painful. In truth, not knowing pervades everything that you do. Will we raise the money in time? Well this time I do believe that we will get the funding. Well we should do. The signs are positive, I think. But we only have a couple of months to do it and in this recession it won't be quick. Should we focus 100% on getting the funding and marketing the business, or should we do some consulting on the side and extend our deadlines? We ought to do the first because it is the most important but the latter seems the most urgent. We make the decision to do one and then the next day I think we should do the other. Why does nothing stand still? And I fear that we will need to do both. It's a case of somehow making them work off each other. Hell, how do I do this all in a day?

Dealing with uncertainty and risk is a key requirement of a great entrepreneur. As William Reeve says: 'Non-entrepreneurs describe entrepreneurs as great risk takers. But this is to misunderstand what good entrepreneurs do. They are working out how to reduce risk. As I once heard someone say: "When I first set it up,

I was stupid. Then, briefly, I was a genius. Once I succeeded, it had always been obvious." To the external world it looks like tons of risk, but the entrepreneur manages away this risk.'

Even on a weekend away in Paris gazing up at the ghostly green light of Notre Dame or watching as the lights on the Eiffel Tower dance like a shimmering 1960s singer, there is no relaxation. The pressing worry of what to do next never quite leaves you. I guess this is why Robert Sapolsky's book *Why Zebras Don't Get Ulcers* is such a funny read. It's so rooted in fact and so scarily accurate on emotions. The author argues that animals out in the wild are less likely to have stress-related illness, because they don't constantly worry about predators. They only worry about lions when they can see them, whereas humans worry constantly about their jobs, relationships or other fears, whether they exist or not, and that leads to ulcers and sickness.

As Ingrid Murray said: 'The worry is that you are one of those businesses who should have given up – what would Dragons' Den say? The Jerry Maguire question "show me the money" is an important reminder.'

Now, a minority of people can deal with this. I remember Matthew Page, manager of Feeder, saying: 'I lock away uncertainty. I stick it in a back cupboard and throw away the key.' That's brilliant if you can do that. But he also admitted that religion plays a role in this. 'I have a lot of faith. I do believe that I am well steered, guided and helped.'

Ingrid said: 'I deal with it in three ways. Firstly in my mind it is a certain. The picture of what success looks like is clear. Secondly I ignore it and just get on with the job at hand. Thirdly it is the uncertainty that is amazing. Creating a new certainty is my value add. Bringing together a range of foods that my mates will buy – not because they're my mates but because they like it. I want to prove that I'm no chicken shit. To be afraid is such a waste. I didn't want to be that person.'

Being positive is key – indeed ideally you enjoy this. As Janie Brown said: 'I like a bit of a risk. I sometimes do like to fly by the seat of my pants. I can deal with this worry. I quite often enjoyed seeing where I landed. I was very optimistic. I enjoy the uncertainty because it can also work positively. You can have some very nice surprises.'

But for the rest, some method of de-stressing is required. Hugo Dixon of Breakingviews says: 'I have done a lot of yoga which helps me deal with stress. You need to have a circuit breaker to slow down. If you don't then you burn out.'

Retaining your sanity throughout this period is tough and some of it just demands sheer willpower. You have to take a deep breath, maybe go outside for some air and then keep going. As Victoria of Pay Check says, 'In the early days of Moneypenny [a previous book-keeping business] I spent a lot of time having no clue about what we were selling. Endless selling off the seat of my pants. I just kept going, I haven't got time to be under the weather or not cope. One simply had to carry on.' Or as Lucy of Lovedean Granola says: 'I don't think about it. When these pitfalls come up I trample over them. I think: I am not letting you stop me.'

There are a number of things that freak most people out and send stress levels through the roof.

This will include the product, people, partnerships, marketing and sales.

Is the product right for the market or have we just not developed it right? It becomes critical to listen and interpret what your customers say. What happens if another competitor launches? Someone's bound to. Every day you watch in trepidation for someone else to appear, but you know rationally that competition is a good thing. It demonstrates traction in the market. So why does a new business freak you out? Well they have VC funding and more people. That's OK. You're doing something different. Aren't you? You ask anyone who will listen. And so it goes on.

What about people – how do you know if you have the right ones? I have hired hundreds of people over the years and you get good at it, but when it's your own money you don't always have the luxury of using headhunters or being able to afford the top salaries, or being able to see a full range of candidates, so you have to improvise. Take time. Don't be forced into a quick decision. Your business will be changing all the time in the early days so you need to be sure you know

> There are a number of things that freak most people out and send stress levels through the roof.

what skills you require from people. Remove the uncertainty by testing people out. Get them to do something for you for free. See if it is any good. Do they fit in and do they understand what you are trying to achieve?

And how do you know whether to progress that partnership opportunity? Should you do it? The temptation is to succumb to a constant 'Tom and Jerry' cartoon battle in your head. 'Well if I do that then I might miss out on a better opportunity and if I don't do that then I may not get another opportunity.'

The critical thing in this continuous barrage of uncertainty is to take decisions and move forward. If you prevaricate on everything because you don't know the answer then you will go mad. You need to have a plan and drive forward. You have to make the best possible decision that you can at the time. As Lucy says: 'It's good sometimes not to vacillate and just to get on with it.' And as Matt Norton of Sentry Wireless says: 'There is only one way to eat an elephant – one bite at a time. Once the strategy has been decided on I resist the temptation to constantly revisit and revise it and force myself to focus on the short-term execution.'

Syzygy nearly merged with another successful web company, Oyster, in 1998, but in the end we decided that we did not share all the same goals and respective views on our mutual worth. We both did well without each other. Instead we went on to merge with a German company, United Media, and I floated the group. Oyster later got bought and has ended up as part of LBi, a large digital agency. Was it the right decision? Who knows and who with hindsight cares? The way to deal with the uncertainty was to keep moving. As long as you keep learning and progressing then you are doing well and the uncertainty won't seem so bad.

You can only go at the pace you can go. Keep your options open. You can't look back. Live with the bloody decision once you have committed to it and move on, whether it works or not. The more decisions you take the luckier you get and in the end the best entrepreneurs make more right decisions than wrong ones!

The life of the start-up is a never-ending mental and physical siege on one's body. It's a massive high but also brings massive lows. There are some clear lessons that one should follow to help cope with this uncertainty:

1 Always have a strategy and plan. You can't make sense of the wider environment and how you fit within it, without this. Adapt and update the plan and execution all the time, but don't ever start out without a strategy and plan.

2 Isolate the unknowns and try to manage away the associated risks in a clear and logical way.

3 Learn to live with your gut instincts. Enjoy the warmth of knowing what is right because you feel it, not because you can rationalise it.

4 Use people to help you. You can't do this alone. People will help. They like to. Talk to people and get it off your chest. The more you talk the better. It's like seeing a shrink. In the end it helps.

5 Do something high risk/high reward. In the end most successful businesses need the wind of word of mouth to grow. If you don't get noticed then nothing will ever happen. Make it happen. Take a calculated risk to give yourself that leg-up. Have some fun and enjoy it. That's infectious.

6 Steal and learn from others. Trust in collective experience. Other people will see what you don't. If it works, then steal it.

7 Make decisions when you need to, but don't worry if you change your mind. You're not driving a FTSE100 board and you don't need to be consistent on everything. In fact the reverse. If you don't drive the business like a racing car, superfast most of the time, but slow occasionally in town, then you won't get anywhere.

8 Have faith. Believe in yourself. Others do, so don't let them down.

Chapter 14
Going with your gut

HOW TO USE YOUR INSTINCTS

Peter Christiansen said to me: 'Good entrepreneurs have a second sense. Their gut feel is always right.'

But what is gut instinct?

It's a feeling. It's a belief. It's not a rational argument.

Nick Wheeler, Founder of Charles Tyrwhitt, says: 'Your gut feeling is all those innermost feelings and those things that have happened in your life and your brain processes them all. Your gut feeling gets better as you get older.'

Bill Gross of Idealab agreed: 'It comes from good information from practice and experience. I like to think that my gut is powerful, but it isn't random. It comes from something – it came from my experiences.'

Starting a business is much closer to nature than running an existing one.

This is why it is so hard for most people, because traditional business rejects anything that isn't rationally based, or supported by customer data or financial metrics. In fact we are all taught to do the reverse of gut instinct, but starting a business is much closer to nature than running an existing one. It's hand to mouth. You often have little information or market data which is the route of all rational analysis. It's survival. It's where do I get my next paycheque or indeed where do I get the first one? Gut instinct plays a fundamental role in the entrepreneur's life. Clearly you use any rational support you can find but the rest becomes instinct. As in nature, you experience new situations all the time that don't fit into a rational framework.

In my experience, women seem better at this than men. I hesitate to generalise, but there's something around accessing feelings here that's crucial to using instinct and the men I know, including myself, struggle with this. Lucy O'Donnell of Lovedean Granola said: 'Women have a more equal balance of gut and rational.' Rather than using feelings, there's a tendency for men to overrationalise – which just gets in the way. Seb James, co-founder of Silverscreen, said: 'I am a total rationalist. Too much – it's probably why I am not a good start-up entrepreneur. I use analytics. I don't see why something that is rational won't work because people don't want it.'

'Having an inner compass is really important,' as Ingrid Murray described it. She also said: 'You need to trust your instinct. At the end of the day if it all goes pear-shaped you only have yourself to blame. Gut instinct is like talent. You either have it or you don't. You either use it or you don't.' Jo Fairley of Green & Black's says: 'The only time I go wrong is when I override my instinct. It is usually to do with people.'

So how do you access this vital skill?

Firstly, you need to be open to it. You need to recognise the fact that you will have strong feelings about your business that don't go away. It's like a sixth sense. It is as though you know something – what is right and wrong – before it has happened or played out. As Hugo Dixon of Breakingviews says, 'It is partly about listening to your emotions. It allows you to free up your intellect.'

Secondly, you need to reflect on times in your career when you felt a decision was wrong, but still went ahead with it. If in the end it turns out that it was a wrong decision, then you should try to recollect why that felt wrong at the time. What were the warning signs that you felt? This is instinct. Similarly you can reflect on decisions that felt right when you made them and later proved to be absolutely the right decision.

When I bought the French company NetForce, as CEO of syzygy, my gut instinct told me that it was a mixed blessing. It massively strengthened our IPO story by allowing us to say that we had strong native companies in the three biggest markets in Europe. NetForce had a good client list, and some good people, but they weren't profitable. Rationally there was no reason why we couldn't get it to make a profit, but I had a nagging feeling that its lack of profitability would come back and bite me. Despite numerous efforts, we could never get the business into continuous profitability. With hindsight I should have waited a bit longer and tried harder to find a profitable company in France that we could do a deal with.

Conversely, when I did not raise all the money I needed for You Wish as a pure consumer proposition, I decided to change our approach and establish a business-to-business model. Instead of trying to create our own consumer business, we would partner with existing brands and offer to provide them with a customised price comparison site which would allow them to cross-sell new services to their customers. We would provide them with the platform for free in return for a share of revenues or profits. When we began to talk to some big household brands about providing them with a specific service in one industry and they really liked the proposition, then I felt vindicated. I had felt for months that I needed a different business model and long before it became clear that I would not raise the funding I needed for the consumer proposition. My decision had been made partly on gut instinct and partly on rational reflection on the difficulties of raising money for pure B2C Internet start-ups, which are much more risky.

Thirdly, you can use rational arguments to support your gut instinct. It's a form of external testing. If you think a person or a partnership

Things obviously have to make sense commercially and therefore rationally, but they also have to *feel* right.

is wrong, then rehearse the objective criteria with someone you trust. See what they think. See if they agree. In the end you find that they generally do agree. Testing your instinct with rational criteria helps to develop your instinct further and soon your feelings can become in synch with what you believe objectively to be the right decision.

Things obviously have to make sense commercially and therefore rationally, but they also have to *feel* right. If all else is equal, and you have done all the sensible and logical things, then using your gut feelings and trusting your instincts can go a long way.

And recognise that in any start-up you can't do everything, as John Bates, Adjunct Professor of Entrepreneurship, London Business School, says: 'The trick is to work out what things to analyse and what things to go with your gut. You only have so much time.'

And gut feeling is something you can use across all elements of a new business. It is not confined to whether you have a good idea or not. Perhaps the most important place to use it is with people. Every time I have hired someone who is good on paper and interviews well, but instinctively I have a nagging doubt about, they don't work out. Even now after many years of hiring people, I can still get it wrong and you know very soon after they have started. It can seem like the lesser of two evils to hire someone who meets some of the spec when you need them, but inevitably it takes longer to deal with the problem that you create. I can remember hiring someone at syzygy. It was an important hire. We were really keen to make the decision and get on with it and yet we just couldn't find the right person for the money we wanted to pay. In the end I decided on someone, but I still had doubts. It just didn't feel right. With hindsight we should have cut our losses but we didn't. We didn't for three years.

Similarly successful partnerships, which are so important to modern business success, are often the result of having positive instincts towards each other as much as rational benefits. This is really true of start-ups. You need to believe in your partners wholeheartedly. Both sides need to feel that they want to commit to making it work. Feelings and emotions are an incredibly important part of the success or failure. When I first started talking to Kennedy Cater (an innovative legal broker) about a partnership, with You Wish bringing the online platform and innovation expertise and them bringing the expertise in the legal industry, I felt it would work.

'Keep focused. Stick to the plan and you'll get there. You'll get the funding you need.'

My wife, Jo, kept reiterating this to me. In truth, I have always known that I would make money out of You Wish. I have always believed that I would crack it. I had spent all the money I had allocated. I was done, but I knew that I would 'bootstrap' my way to the finishing line.

Not every business I have been involved with

has felt like this. You can hope and you can pray, but deep down you know whether you will make it. You can sense it. It's a strange thing to say, but as an entrepreneur you learn to use your feelings and instincts in a way that many business people never do.

So how do you learn to use your gut instinct?

1 Feel more. Don't just rationalise and think. Ask yourself what you actually feel about an issue. Then speak the answer out loud as if you really feel and mean it. Sometimes it can be surprising what you actually say you feel. It can be different to what you think.

2 Reflect on the decisions that you have taken that were strongly positive or negative. Remember what you felt at the time and try to link those feelings with the eventual decisions. See what they tell you. It's not mumbo jumbo, it works. Human instincts are strong and can be deployed in business even in the twenty-first century.

3 When the lights go out, do you believe in your own business and dream? If the answer is no then you have problems. Everyone has doubts and fears but ultimately you have to feel that your business is going to be a success. Try to fix the problem. If you think you can fix it over time then you'll be fine, but if you feel it's a fundamental flaw then really ask yourself whether you should continue.

Chapter 15 Finding your North Star

HOW TO CREATE A VISION THAT PEOPLE CAN SHARE

'You believed that we would float syzygy and we believed you. We all felt part of something amazing. We knew that it would succeed.'

Jonathan, formerly technical director at syzygy, said this to me years after syzygy floated on the German Stock Exchange. It surprised me. Firstly that we all obviously had such unshakeable belief in what we were doing and where we were going. Secondly that we ever floated the company, given that revenues were only €18m at that stage and that so few small/medium-sized companies ever do go public successfully. And yet it did happen. We just aimed for it. Every time we reviewed company progress, we reiterated that it was our goal to

IPO the company. Somehow it became the North Star that we followed, the guiding principle that drove us.

And it is easy to forget how powerful a group of people can be when they are united around a vision, a cause or a leader. I can remember the buzz that existed, the sense of walking tall when we said who we were. I felt exhilarated all the time. I felt triumphal at the head of an unstoppable army. We had pride in good publicity and good work, but also the fact that we were very profitable at a time when most of our competitors were not.

If you don't have a strong sense of where you are going, then starting a business can be a gruesome affair. No money, stress, exhaustion and despair. When you have a purpose, that means a lot to you and to others, then you are much more likely to deliver it. You can share it. It becomes your religion. It gives you the strength to carry on. And if you carry on then others follow.

> When you have a purpose, then you are much more likely to deliver it. It becomes your religion.

But creating a vision or a dream or a belief set is not easy. It can be particularly difficult when the business is doing something new, something different and when it is still germinating. Visions can be either driving thoughts or purposes like revolutionising the airline industry with low-cost travel or they can be simply goals, like floating a business or becoming the UK's largest. One is not necessarily better than the other, but they are very different. Driving thoughts can be much tougher as they often involve changing things or markets and so have much less clarity early on. Conversely visions that are based on financial or market size often have less emotional edge but can still be very motivating to people, especially if there is financial reward tied into their attainment.

When eSubstance (as it was called then) started out, it was going to be the leading provider of branded offline content on the web. It was compelling enough for us to raise over £10m in investment from 3i in 2000 but it quickly became clear that creating online content from offline sources was not a sustainable or profitable model. We wavered and wandered across all industry sectors, looking for a purpose for several years as we spent our way through the money. The vision began to fade. It was only when we bought a small contract publisher, Ink, who were producing easyJet's magazine that we finally found our way. We were then able to re-orientate the vision and eventually we became the world's leading contract publisher of in-flight media.

As Jeffrey O'Rourke says: 'You have to be passionate. You need a growth vision. A vision of how the market will grow. How you have assembled a constellation of people and ways that you are adding value that has not existed before. This compels people. When you're very enthusiastic, people have a hard time resisting.'

Roland Rudd of Finsbury Communications said he set out a vision for his PR company: 'Within five years to be in the top five, within the next five years to be in the top two and within the next five to be number one.' And he has achieved it!

Companies with visions can often find they run into problems when their original vision doesn't quite work out the way they wanted. This can be as true for a plumber as it is for a new bank. Often it falters because the underlying proposition or idea that needs to make money doesn't work and so the vision is cut off from something that pays the bills. In all cases success comes from having a simple compelling proposition that customers want to pay for and that can be delivered profitably. If this proposition is also tied into something with a higher purpose, a human meaning, then it can really take off, but it's hard to achieve.

We started You Wish with what we thought was a really clear purpose. We wanted to help busy people with families and careers get their unmet needs met, and therefore have more fulfilled lives. We saw how many busy people never had time to search for hours to find services they needed and so just never did. We all suffer from endless to-do lists. We saw the opportunity in reversing the typical marketplace so that if you gave some information about who you are and what you want then companies would be delighted to send you personal responses. But as we developed, it became clear that the vision was too big and disparate for our financial resources. We were trying to achieve too much. This is why we didn't get it right to start with. The business has just not been clear enough. Shit! How did that happen? Some people were using it to get information, some to find products and others to find services. We could not cover every area and after all there were some rather large and hairy competitors who did much of this better than we could. This has made us refocus the business. The vision may remain but it needs money to bring it to life.

It is worth noting that while the vision and story may seem similar, they have very different roles. The vision is your goal – where you want the business to end up. The story is how you are going to get there and why you will achieve that. They are both extremely important.

Clarity can be just as important as anything. As Victoria Baillieu of Pay Check said: 'Everybody can be inspired. People like strong leadership. Everybody buys in to the fact that we do one service very well. If there is a problem the founders will pick it up. They are inspired by the fact that we are leading from the front. People have seen the benefit of hard work. They know that we would go back to licking stamps if we had to.'

In fact it doesn't have to be original – it just has to be simple and full of passion. As Nick Wheeler, founder of Charles Tyrwhitt, says: 'I want to create a great business. I want our customers, our people, our suppliers to love the business. I don't want to sell the business. This is like my fifth child. You don't run them forever,

> The vision is your goal. The story is how you are going to get there. They are both extremely important.

but you don't sell them. It's a simple story. I want it to be great and I don't want to sell it.'

Another avenue to explore when you are trying to crystallise your vision is to leverage other people and partners. If people say they really like what you are doing, and yet you are still not getting the traction that you ought to, then keep thinking on the problem. Keep working on the purpose and keep listening to what people say. The more customers talk positively about a facet of the business, the more you see the real traction. Equally look for partners to help scale what you are doing. Once you see what a partner aspires to leverage then you also start to learn what the real value of what you are doing is. The epicentre of your vision is the combination of what your customers, friends and partners say they value.

So how do you create that vision that drives people?

1 Be passionate. Be emotional about what you are doing – why is it important? Why should people care? Find the emotional bond that binds you and your business to others.

2 Be clear and simple. Don't give up looking for the vision. Keep testing out your thoughts. When they click, people will tell you immediately. They will relate to what you are saying.

3 Make it a shared dream. Make sure that all the people who are working on the business or project are engaged with it. Link them into the success. This is more about bringing to life what good looks like than it is about giving them financial rewards.

4 Recruit believers. They will already be emotionally engaged. And make sure that they are the best people. Then you have brilliant believers!

5 Find partners – companies who can help you achieve your vision, who see what you see.

6 Weave your vision into your story. Give it a compelling endgame. Give evidence of your success in getting there through that story.

Chapter 16
Don't spare
the rod

HOW TO DEAL WITH FEAR, FAILURE AND REJECTION

'Is it worth it?' Billie, my therapist, says to me as I sit in an all too familiar armchair in her tiny study.

I know she thinks I am missing the point. I know she wonders why I continue to work so hard at the expense of everything when it doesn't even seem to make me happy and it isn't making me money yet.

How do I explain why it's so important? It just is. I just can't fail.

The problem is that fear of failure is worse than failure. It gnaws at you day and night. It challenges you to do better. It's the Catholic cilice or spiked leather belt of *Da Vinci Code* fame – unsettling, painful sometimes, an unwelcome presence lurking ominously, a shadow over early spring thoughts. Every day you have to kick yourself into action like a recalcitrant engine – oil won't do. You have to think positive and keep painting a bright and sunny picture. Conversely failure is done and dusted and you can't change it. The mind learns to move on. It's a healing thing the doctors say.

Business books seem to give conflicting advice on how to deal with rejection and failure. Some say you must not countenance it at all. Others say use it and learn from it. Most serial entrepreneurs swear by using its power positively. But either way it takes time and mental stamina to control it. Peter Christiansen said: 'The single most important emotion is lack of emotion. You need to be thick-skinned.'

Vaughan Smith dealt with it by giving himself no other way out. As he said, 'By burning our boats, the horror of failure was so great, we never considered the option of failure. It was survival. I never conceived of life where it did not work.'

When we did not raise the money for On the Frontline, I took it really personally. It felt like I was a failure but the reality is that there wasn't a business model and we were too early for video. I was in love with the idea and although people found it fascinating, it couldn't fly without a lot of money. I didn't realise this at the time but now I do.

Every time you start a business, you learn another set of business lessons and they are not very difficult to remember. If you don't have a proper business model – a way of making money

– then it won't work. If there is no significant customer problem or pain or demand then nobody will buy what you are selling. If you can't get your products or services in front of your audience then you lack a proper go-to-market strategy. And so on and so forth. You also learn how to recognise this in any business idea. But learning how to cope with rejection and failure takes more time. It's not a rational exercise.

> Learning how to cope with rejection and failure takes more time. It's not a rational exercise.

You need to take the positives out of these learnings. As Ingrid Murray says: 'I am an optimist. Things that you may class as a failure – I don't see them that way. My new business, WeBuyNearby, has a much better start because of the mistakes I have learned from along the way.'

In fact some entrepreneurs approach this by actively welcoming failure. As Mark de Wesselow, co-founder of Square Meal, said: 'You must expect a few failures. We have perhaps run our business too cautiously. You must accept that failures help make you stronger and better able to cope with problems going forward.'

Bill Gross, founder of Idealab, sums it up well when he says: 'How you deal with uncertainty and failure *is* the difference between success and failure. It has got to be part of the fabric of every company. If you deal with adversity as a challenge, or just another hill to climb over then you will survive. I don't know how to flick that switch in someone. I don't know how you get it. It's not necessarily smarts or ambition. It's how you deal with adversity. You do something heroic to overcome it. Disney faced adversity. If the magical Disney struggled we all will.

'Success is not a good teacher. Failure is a much better teacher. You just have to imagine you took a very expensive class! Then you really pay attention. It's not like three years at college when you don't pay any attention at all.'

Over an evening drink one day my brother said to me: 'What's the worst thing that can happen to you if it doesn't work?'

I couldn't believe he thought that. I sure as hell couldn't believe that he said it. Did he really think that I would fail after everything that I had done and worked for? I really hated this. It could have been anyone else but actually I really hated my brother saying this to me. It felt like if he said it, then everyone must think it. Everyone must think that I had screwed it up. It made me squirm. It made me angry, determined and nervous at the same time.

'I'd get another job,' I eventually said to him.

He was trying to put it all into perspective at a time when I hadn't raised the money for the original consumer idea. He was trying to help, but it's easy to take everything negatively when you are feeling down, when you feel it's not working.

And it's also about adapting quickly when failure comes, as John Bates, Adjunct Professor of Entrepreneurship, London Business School, says: 'Expect failure. It is the norm. The real question is how you spot it before it happens. If it isn't working then stop and change.'

I remember that for some time after I bought

NetForce as a French office for the syzygy group, I fretted about the decision. Given that the rest of our group made money, it didn't seem like a difficult task to turn it round. We had a plan and we would execute it, but I just couldn't make it work. I tried everything. For a while it seemed to be turning the corner and then wham, it was losing money again. It felt like I had failed. I had made a mistake. It took time to realise two important lessons. I should have asked others more experienced than me to help ensure it was the right choice – after all I had never bought a business before. Secondly we were incredibly short of time to get a deal done. There were only so many options available. In future I would learn to question the strategy rather than make a hasty decision that might be wrong. And equally it is easy to focus on the negatives rather than the positives – I had successfully floated the business for €240m!

Strangely failure and learnings also give you more confidence in your own abilities. Nick Wheeler of Charles Tyrwhitt said: 'We went bust in '94. We got legged over by a supplier. Effectively an agent. There were eight of us. It felt like the world had collapsed. It felt like my entire working life had collapsed. There was a moment of total despair. The receiver threw us out and we went to the pub in Munster Road. I stood up in front of my seven staff and burst into tears. Then I thought: this is my business – it will work. It is all about self-belief and making it happen. We bought ourselves back out again.

> Strangely failure and learnings also give you more confidence in your own abilities.

My father mortgaged his house and he lent me the money. He did it because it was a good business. He made it a commercial loan. We paid it back in six months. It focused the mind and it was a real lesson in trusting people. We got rid of the agent. I came out thinking I will never trust anyone again. It is not the case but I do think very hard before I trust anyone. I want to live by my own actions. If I do well I want to shine.'

And sometimes little things can have an unexpectedly large impact on you and your self-esteem. I have spent most of my working life in an office environment. I love them. I actually thrive on being with lots of people, so if you start working from home it can be a real shock to the system. In fact unless you have to change the way you work, then don't do it. I can feel the fear of giving up my office to bootstrap our way through to funding. The thought of working again from home freaked me out. It seemed to say failure. It meant that I did not have a shiny office, PA and all the normal accoutrements of success. Yet some people love working from home and never want to work in an office again. They love the freedom of working to their own time. And then one day it happened, I had not raised the funding yet and I had to pull the plug on the office and move back home. I had to have Nick and Claire working with me in my home office. Fuck, my pride hurt. But fuck your pride. After all nobody cares. You just need to prove them wrong. You need to accept that you may lose the odd battle and just move on.

There are some key lessons that will help you deal with rejection and failure. They often sound obvious until you're in the thick of it and appreciate any kind of help!

1 Channel your reaction to failure as a positive not as a negative thought. Use it to answer the question what will I now do better, not what should I have done better. Don't dwell on the specific failure and when it was triggered; instead learn from the events and activities that caused that failure. Learn from specifics like how not to spend money and progress. Learn that there are always ways to cut corners if you look for them. So focus on finding them, not moaning about what is dead and buried.

2 Use every mistake as a way to learn about how to manage money better and how to make smarter choices about what you spend your money on.

3 Rationalise each failing. Don't emotionalise them as a personal problem. Share them with others so that they help you to do this.

4 Don't make the same mistakes twice. Let failures make you a better judge.

5 Understand your own negative trigger points and avoid them. If you can't stand doing things on your own, then don't start a business without a partner. It sounds so obvious and yet

many make the same mistakes time and again. They do things that their basic character cannot cope with.

6 Focus on doing things that suit your skills and experience. It's easy to fall in love with an idea, but it'll be easier and more rewarding if you choose something that combines your passion, experience and skills.

7 Have self-belief. Don't do it if you don't.

Part 4
Dusk or dawn

IT'S GOING ONE WAY OR THE OTHER.

Either you're starting to feel like the worst is over and it's looking brighter, or you're feeling disillusioned. Either you're making money or you're not. Either the dream is coming true or you might need to get another job and go back to the drawing board. Whichever one it is, you need a plan to deal with it. And you need to deal with the inevitable emotions that will accompany your heaven or hell.

Whichever way it is going, you're not out of the woods just yet. You will need to focus hard on some key areas now to get to the finishing line:

- How do you make your team work? How do you make them world class?

- How do you deal with the fact that you might be running out of money?

- What happens if it's really not working and your mind is flooded with doubts? How do you know whether you should keep going or cut your losses? How do you take the decision to kill your baby, to kill this dream that you have lived, loved and hated for so much time?

- What do you do when it all starts to work? How do you keep it coming? How do you enjoy it? How do you avoid blowing it?

- What do you do when all the lights have really gone out and you're in a financial and emotional mess?

- How do you get your first homerun? How do you safely ensure you leave the start-up phase behind?

A crucial part of this stage is ensuring that you are building up your team and extending the business out from the founders to incorporate new talents and ideas.

Chapter 17 Building the right family

HOW DO YOU CREATE A WINNING TEAM?

'Jane is pregnant! We've decided to make a go of it. We'd like your support. Is that going to be a problem?'

Jim, a business colleague, had taken me in to our meeting room to tell me this in private.

'No, of course it's not. That's brilliant. I am delighted for you both,' I said genuinely, masking my initial surprise and pondering whether it had happened in our offices.

The truth is when you start a business, you start a family with all the excitement and emotions that this brings. At the beginning it's just the founders and you're still in the early stages of marriage, but as the relationship develops, so you take on staff. Sometimes your staff work from your home and they have a weirdly intimate exposure to every aspect of your life. And whether you're all working from someone's home or in your small start-up office, you are living on top of each other. It's completely different to running a large business.

Founders never have all the right skills, however well you plan. Early hires become critical. Now it's a trueism to say that these new people are expected to work hard, often for very little cash, but they play another critical role in helping the start-up succeed. They bring new thinking and perspectives, a divergence of ideas and different skills. Their energy provides emotional stimulus. You all work together. It's all hands to the pump. I can see an image of five or six of us in the early days of syzygy working very late in the office. Our first two proper developers were pounding on their keyboards with kebabs and chips dripping grease everywhere. They had infectious smiles as they coded merrily away deep into the night and we were all happy, united in our purpose. The business equivalent of a late-night family dinner in the kitchen.

But how do you choose the right early employees? It's so critical to get these hires right. Not only do you pay with poor work if you choose the wrong ones, but you also infect the company with a bad emotional vibe. People know faster than you when you make the wrong decision.

As Peter Christiansen said, 'It's very hard to realise you have mediocre people. Brilliant people are easy to spot.'

Pick 'originals'. Pick people who are brilliant and not just good. Every time you pick someone special it has an extraordinarily explosive effect on the business. Their talents and skills boost the whole operation exponentially. They see things that you don't. They inspire in ways that you can't replicate. But they should have the same values as the founders. They must have certain emotional traits. They must be people who see the world through 'the glass half full'. They must be givers and not takers. They should bring energy, enthusiasm and determination to everything that they do.

They'll deliver for you if they have natural talent and you let it grow. You can't repress or restrict their natural behaviours. But you also have to nurture it. Strong families support each other through thick and thin and so it is in the early days of a start-up. You have to go the extra mile for your people when they need your support. I remember one person, Paul, a project manager, would literally ask me questions all day long, sucking knowledge from me. Some days it was relentless and I had no time to do enough of my own tasks, and really felt like telling him to get lost, but actually the investment in

> Pick people who are brilliant and not just good. Every time you pick someone special it has an extraordinarily explosive effect on the business.

his understanding paid off as he quickly took on new responsibilities and problems. Indeed his interest and preparedness to learn was an incredibly strong value in the company, and he has become a lifelong friend. We all shared a determination to learn, experiment and be better and that has real value as a start-up. You have to keep experimenting because you haven't found your natural rhythm yet.

As Greg Hadfield, co-founder of Soccernet, said, 'It was strange with Tom. When he was 12, I was relentless at playing the father and 12-year-old son card. People wanted that story. Tom did a lot of work to start with. There was a tension because I didn't have the skills and Tom didn't want to be my employee. At the age of 17 he went to Davos. In the end I allowed him to lead a normal teenage life!'

> You also have to take time out to ensure everyone is on the same page and understands where the company is trying to go.

You also have to take time out to ensure everyone is on the same page and understands where the company is trying to go. This provides an opportunity for both concentrated work and play. I remember at syzygy in the early days we took over a cheap but unusual Landmark Trust house, with its own bowling alley, for a few days as a small team. The first night provided the inevitable bonding session. It was punctuated by too much drink and then the bowling and then someone threw up all over the nineteenth-century wooden skittles! This type of event provides the company with its early history. These stories become enhanced corporate folklore over time. People who were there get a kick out of telling them and people who joined later like to sit round the 'camp fire' and hear them again. It builds a strong culture and cultures build successful companies.

In the good months the family grows and everyone prospers, but like all human dramas it has its ups and downs. First one of the star employees wants to move on. You just don't yet have the full set of commercial opportunities or size to hold them as they want to learn fast. It's killing. There is nothing you can do except wish them well and remember the good things that they have done to help you move forward. And then there are the disagreements over strategy, what is important and what isn't. Sometimes being transparent doesn't equally give you the answers that you want. I remember a syzygy session of ten of us in the early days. The plan was to get everybody pushing in the right direction but the truth was that some of the original hires just wanted to go in a different direction. And in the end they left one after another. It was like a divorce. When three people leave a tiny start-up it robs the business of so much knowledge and cultural history. It can feel like a crippling blow. It is really painful. So much effort wasted, but you just have to keep going. The family has to move on.

Sometimes the early performers just can't evolve with the business, as Seb James of Silverscreen said: 'There is a difference between what you need and what you can afford. You end up with people you ought not to have done.

Our operations director got to 50 stores but then couldn't get it further. We had to take him out. It was a betrayal but we had no real choice.'

So as you evolve, it helps to be very clear about roles, to find the right people and manage performance closely. As William Reeve of LOVEFiLM says: 'We bought out the management as we took over businesses. Then we started recruiting professionals including the CEO. We then recruited all the other heads. I put a lot of store by people management. We had management by objective and performance related pay. It was a quarterly management performance system. It's a bit bureaucratic but it's transparent and it works.'

And there are times when the culture nurtured early on becomes a massive barrier to growth, as Sue van Meeteren of Jigsaw said: 'Ann's husband calls it the Democratic Republic of Jigsaw. For six or seven years everything was taken by majority decision. We were rebelling against Research International. No job titles. But in the end we lacked grit in the oyster. And bit by bit we have taken power back.' It requires constant attention to herd the family in the right direction and keep it moving forward.

This can become doubly difficult when the parents argue. They can have ferocious arguments in full view of the children. It's not good for anyone but it's often just the way it is. I can remember John Hunt and I arguing furiously over the new syzygy website on Christmas Eve. None of the office could believe

> There are times when the culture nurtured early on becomes a massive barrier to growth.

that so much anger and angst could be spilled when so few people were likely to be looking at it in those early days of the web. With hindsight it was just taken out of proportion, but that happens in families.

It's also important to leverage everyone's different strengths and use them appropriately and there really are differences, as Bill Gross of Idealab says: 'Female entrepreneurs have very good instincts about people, when they're lying or when people are not being ethical. Male entrepreneurs could learn from watching how women do this. I don't know what it is, but females in our company have very strong instincts that turn out to be right. Maybe they watch people's body language more and how that matches what they say. I don't know how, but they are better at it!'

But it works both ways: men also have skills that women would benefit from learning or using more. As Bill Gross says: 'Males have a tendency to say things with such authority that they persuade people, they take them with them. Yet at the end you still go wow how did they do that? Females are sometimes shy and don't use such conviction to persuade people. They might do better by having more of that assumptive style.'

And then sometimes there are the events that you can never expect, like death!

'When Feeder's drummer killed himself it was mortifying. I had prided myself on building a family. I wasn't the type that wanted to be out at industry events. I drove our family through the heavily congested highway of the music industry. It was our vehicle. And then in front of us the worst thing that could happen, happened – a suicide. I felt he let us down. And I felt we let him down. It killed us in the US. I had to go into overdrive. I had a stiff upper lip. With hard work we got through it. All my military training kicked in,' said Matthew Page, manager of Feeder.

Of course on other occasions you are all celebrating success and early victories. These are the first milestones of the business. They provide the fodder that the emerging family will remember with pride as the business expands.

So what lessons should you remember if you want to create that winning family?

1 Go the extra mile for every one of them. In the same way that parents shouldn't have favourites, so you should give support to all and every one of them. Find time to answer their questions, give them the training they need and provide emotional support and they will repay tenfold.

2 Create one unit, one team, one family. Take time out together and encourage them to support each other. In time they will take ownership and responsibility for issues that you never even envisaged.

3 Make them part of the story. Delegate to them. Give them responsibility beyond their age and talent. Let them be the heroes.

4 Deliver the things that you promise to them, and otherwise don't promise stuff. They won't necessarily expect a lot, after all you are a start-up, but if you are going to make extravagant gestures then you better keep to them.

5 If someone doesn't fit in then cut them loose to protect the family. Be ruthless in your focus on keeping the core unit fit and happy. You're the lion and this is your jungle!

Chapter 18
In the red or in the black

HOW DO YOU COPE WITH GAMBLING YOUR MONEY
AWAY?

'You can't keep spending. You've got to put a final figure on how much you are going to invest and then *not* go over it. You just can't. You just can't spend all our house money. It's not fair.'

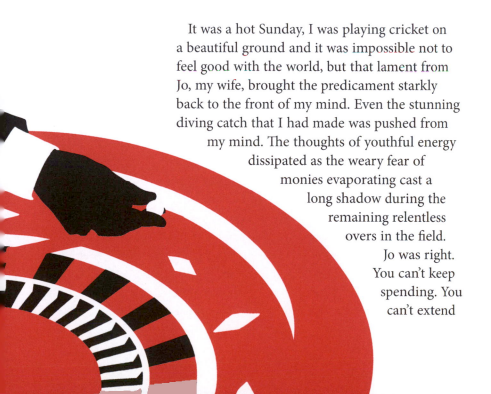

It was a hot Sunday, I was playing cricket on a beautiful ground and it was impossible not to feel good with the world, but that lament from Jo, my wife, brought the predicament starkly back to the front of my mind. Even the stunning diving catch that I had made was pushed from my mind. The thoughts of youthful energy dissipated as the weary fear of monies evaporating cast a long shadow during the remaining relentless overs in the field. Jo was right. You can't keep spending. You can't extend the deadline multiple times. There has to be a finite amount of money you throw at an idea, even if it is more than you said originally. Then if you can't make it happen, you should just stop. But it was so close. It must get to the next stage – the investment that I knew I could get.

I started out with a figure that I was prepared to spend. It was a lot of money – a proper six-figure sum. I was prepared to give up my CEO role where I was also getting a six-figure sum. But I never envisaged for one moment that I wouldn't get the funding that I knew that I needed. It was just a question of time. I was comfortable spending the money – it was an investment in the future. I knew that I would make it.

But now that set sum of money was gone. We had made a bit of revenue along the way, but not enough. I had hit the end of the road. And we just happened to be in the biggest recession of our lives. Fuck – what timing. The thing is you can't change horses once you have started out on the road.

In the early days of the project I had never minded spending the money, as I had made a decision over a long period of time to take this gamble. In fact curiously I was quite happy paying bills on a quiet Sunday morning as I listened to classical music, But as time went on I began to resent paying out money to other people and not paying myself any. What had seemed so brilliant – namely that I invested most of the money and had most of the equity – now pissed me off as I paid my business partner Nick's salary each month. Time passed on and things took longer than envisaged, as they always do, but I was confident that I would get the money so didn't panic. It was only when I had spent 80% of the money that the fear began to creep in. Actually it was two types of fear, both cold and incessant. The first was the fear that I had wasted so much energy, money and passion, which I could have better applied to something else. Maybe I could have made a better financial investment, maybe a better investment of effort and maybe a better career investment. The second was that I might have to keep spending over my limit. How far would that be and how would I cope with that?

That's the trouble, you have invested so much you don't want to give it up. You believe that just a little more will get you there. This is really true when it's your money. When someone else has put the money in, then it's simple. If they pull the plug you're dead, but if it's all your own money then only you are the plug puller! Only you control your destiny. It's only a little more. And then you look round and all about you are the roulette tables and the chances to make it all work. It's an addiction. You feel the need to feed it, to keep going, to keep your dream alive. But as with all gambles in the end there is a time and a place and you can only spend so much.

I spent money badly. You don't need to spend £20k on a brand identity that you never use because you change the name! How bloody

> As with all gambles in the end there is a time and a place and you can only spend so much.

stupid can you get and what would I do now for that £20k? And what about that last piece of market research which we never really exploited? One of the first things you need to learn is to economise. You may have saved up some money to do this, but that's irrelevant. This is on your wallet now and not on someone else's. Don't spend money on things unless you are sure that you need them. And don't spend money on people unless you absolutely have to. Make people sweat for you like you are doing personally. Think and rethink if there is some other way to achieve what you want without spending money. Anticipate things that you will need and give yourself time to find cheaper ways to pay for them. Your ability to be smart with how you spend your money will help you cope with gambling on your baby.

Your ability to be smart with how you spend your money will help you cope with gambling on your baby.

And you're not alone. Losing money is a great lesson for an entrepreneur. As Nick Wheeler of Charles Tyrwhitt says: 'I put in £70,000 and lost it. I then realised that you can't do it the VC way. It is very easy to spend money you haven't made. So I just settled down as a tortoise. For the first few years I lived on nothing. You can live on nothing.'

Or as John Bates, Adjunct Professor of Entrepreneurship, London Business School, says: 'People need to expect to lose money. The median return on early stage business is 0%. This is why even VCs don't do it!'

Secondly look for alternatives to everything. Anticipate that the first part of your investment won't deliver exactly what you need. You will need more money or more resources. Focus on extending your runway, and on giving yourself extra room to manoeuvre. Ultimately if you haven't got the additional money to invest then you will need alternative routes. You will need to find a different way of moving forward. This may be investors or partners who do things for you in return for equity or a share of future profits. Again, your ability to craft different solutions will give you some comfort at this traumatic time.

And don't assume that it will generate you exactly what you planned. As Janie Brown said: 'To base your children's education on fickle buyers is a ludicrous thing to do. I did it, but I had no fall back.'

I have been in that situation that many entrepreneurs run into. I didn't have the money to keep moving forward as I needed to, but I knew what the right next move should be. The trouble is without investment I was nowhere and yet getting investment without creating more traction was difficult. This is the classic 'hamster on a wheel' predicament. I was so painfully close. Only the day before Olivier, a corporate financier and colleague from Edengene, the strategy and innovation consultancy I ran, had repeated to me the words that I told him some months before: 'I agree someone is going to make big money out of what you are doing, the question is only whether it will be you!' What a red rag to a bull. I had to find the money. I had to raise the funding. I had to find a way. Olivier had pushed me. He said: 'Go and raise it first from your friends and family – they are the ones who believe in you. Do it. They won't mind investing £20,000 on you, even if you end up losing it all, as long as you gave it your best shot.' But now I would be into a different game, gambling my friends' money. It happened to me in 2000 when I floated syzygy on the Neuer Markt and made a lot of money. Both my brother and father had put in a lot of money at the IPO price and because of the dotcom crash, both of them lost money on it, in spite of the fact that we raised a lot of money. Not something one feels good about.

Thirdly manage financial risk away as much as possible. As William Reeve of LOVEFiLM said: 'In my first business, a research business, we had no money. We had been going a year and had seven or eight staff. We decided to launch a conference. To launch that conference we had to commit to £50k of investment in advance. If we failed we would have gone out of business. But by the time we made the commitment we had reduced the risk hugely by researching it intricately and preparing a very detailed plan that we were very confident would work – and, as it turned out, it did.'

And sometimes this means going slower than people tell you! As Jo Fairley of Green & Black's says: 'We had some serious financial crunches. But we knew that the business was worth something and we weren't going to go under. It was always cashflow. It was having to finance massive amounts of stock. 20–30% growth is probably sustainable. Everyone thinks 100% p.a. growth is fantastic, but it's going to give you seriously sleepless nights!' It can be counter-intuitive, but sometimes growing more slowly and in a more controlled way gives you more options. If you don't have external funding this cash flow requirement may become a big problem. Green & Black's might well have survived on its own for longer without private equity, if the cashflow requirements hadn't got so extreme.

Finally have belief. This emotion does play such an important role in so many parts of the entrepreneur's life. As Ingrid Murray said; 'I don't think many single mums with four kids would have gambled the way I have, but I had to be true to myself. I have spent £70–80k that I didn't have. The biggest cost is that I haven't earned money for a year. But I am task-driven. I can see it. I am living the success of it, but worrying that it might not work … I can dare to believe that it will work. This is the first thing that I have done that I think the timing is right. It is me and its manifestation. I take more risk than most people. I am deluded.'

And you need to match certainty with belief if you really want to exploit all the opportunities and that can mean taking some risks. As Claire Mason of PR company, Man Bites Dog, admits: 'I don't like financial uncertainty. I like to have control. Fear of failure is a massive driver. I will

> You need to match certainty with belief if you really want to exploit all the opportunities and that can mean taking some risks.

go to any lengths to avoid it. You could argue that our growth and profitability curve has been a little too perfect – which means I am not taking enough risk. We probably need a bit of drama!'

There are always compromises that have to be made when it comes to money and start-ups. It is rarely straightforward. The critical thing is to find a way to keep making progress because that relieves your stress and demonstrates to you and others that it is worthwhile.

There are ways to mitigate some of the fear and stress and cope better as you gamble your future:

1 Economise from day one. Assume that you will run out of money. Don't assume that you will raise any money. Assume that you need to conserve money and be as tight as you can on everything. I know this now, as I didn't do it. I am a spender by nature and not a saver. That is a bad mix for an entrepreneur starting his or her own business. So learn to change.

2 Leverage the incredible free resources that now exist for entrepreneurs online from software of every type for timesheets, project management, accounts to training, to seminars, etc.

3 Work on the key financial success metrics from day one – assume that you need to have lots of escape routes and options and follow them all up.

4 Fix on a sum that you are prepared to spend and add a 30% contingency. Then aim to spend no more than 50% of the core amount without the contingency. Then when you spend the original amount faster than you thought, you still have a significant buffer. 10% is not enough!

5 Focus on sales from day one. Try to get early revenue. It makes the sun shine and keeps the chill wind of despair at bay!

Chapter 19
Killing your baby

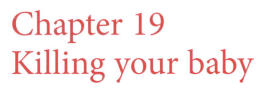

HOW DO YOU
KNOW WHEN
TO CALL
TIME, IF YOUR
BUSINESS IS NOT WORKING?

The old adage 'You can put lipstick on a pig, but it's still a pig' can be sadly relevant for your most treasured possession, your new business!

There are times when the kindest thing that you can do for yourself is to kill that baby, that new-found business. If it isn't working and if it isn't going to work, then there is no point in dawdling; just be merciful and put the wounded animal out of its misery.

Once it became clear that turning round syzygy's French office, NetForce, was not going to be easy, if even possible, then there was no point waiting. It felt so tough to do this, after all the time invested in buying it and working with it. But in the end the sooner we took the tough decision the sooner we would be better off for it. The business was sold to the French MD but he couldn't make it work either!

You can often limp along, not really making any money and not really losing any money.

The problem is that you can often limp along, not really making any money and not really losing any money. You have got insufficient resources and self-belief to drive the business to a new place or the market may just be too negative. Either way it is emotionally and psychologically exhausting. It really is better for you to close it down.

But how do you do this?

It's difficult to do, I know. You have spent hours, days, weeks, months and even years writing plans, talking to people, selling it, getting people on board. It's been a real rush, so much fun at times, so scary at others, and all wrapped in a big blanket of hope and self-belief. It's been your dream. And then there are all those other people who have been involved; people that you have got close to, who you have bonded with to help you move it forward. Every time you think about being brutal about it, you find ways to prevaricate, to try another route, to give it one more moment of life.

Seb James said, when Silverscreen had 65 stores and a £65m turnover but was still haemorrhaging cash: 'When you can see the burn, you can predict the day you go bust. If you are operationally leveraged there is not much you can do to release the cash. You sort of know, but humans are resilient. You find a solution. There are grandiose ways to raise the phoenix from the ashes. We all live in hope.'

Seb's business had been pole-axed by three different factors in the mid 2000s: entertainment retail was a dead concept, it got caught in a war between supermarkets, the Internet and specialist entertainment software (they started ripping the margin out of Silverscreen's catalogue), and newspapers started giving DVDs away for free.

Seb said: 'I remember lying in the bath and hauling myself out to face another fucking day. You have to show your people that all is OK. You shut the door with your partners and then you have to come out and talk about the plans. You are perpetually living a lie.'

In the end Apax, a venture capitalist, pulled the plug on the business. Ultimately someone has to pull the plug – whether it's you or your investors.

There are some key steps that you have to go through to kill your baby – this is like an addiction; if you don't wean yourself off it, you can get into real difficulties:

1. Firstly you have to recognise that it won't work or that you can't make it work. Yes it could limp along for a while, but there is no satisfaction in that. It's better to go and do something else than to continue with something that is failing.
2. Then you have to stop working on it and certainly stop spending any money on it. It's the start-up version of going to the clinic for a detox!
3. Thirdly you have to start thinking about doing something else.

4. Then you have to close it all down, or sell or give it to someone else.
5. Finally you actually have to start doing something else.

When you make the decision to close it, then give yourself time to do some productive things. For example, Seb and his business partner Ernesto helped to find jobs for many of the people in their head office – it provided a respite from the gloom.

When do you know the right time to kill your baby?

If you sense that you are coming to the end of the road, or you just can't seem to make any headway, or you're running out of money, then ask experienced people that you trust for an honest answer about the state of your company and the opportunity. Force them to tell you what they really think. You don't want platitudes. You want the truth even if you can't handle it. You need to know if they think it's a dumb idea to keep it going. You also need to know if they think it's a good idea but you don't have the means or skills to make it work. Either way they both lead to the same conclusion – that it is time to stop what you are doing.

You may also need help to close it down. As Janie Brown of Jane Brown Shoes said: 'I was worried about Paul. We were very close to the wire – everything was vulnerable. Just in the nick of time we met our business mentor. We were thinking of raising more money. Our mentor said: "Stop! Paul, you need to work separately from this business – it won't work with you two as business partners." To me he said you are first and foremost a designer and not a business woman. Stop your business, take a break and look at it again with fresh eyes.'

But there are times when you can see a way through even if you have to kill what you have spent ages slaving over and start again but in a different direction. You can see a Houdini-like escape from your predicament. As Matt Norton said: 'It was difficult. It was a huge emotional and financial investment, in our case made more difficult because we believe the end user proposition was right. We had started with parental control on the phone with a SIM firewall, but it wasn't scalable. We put it into life support and put all our efforts into a new strategic focus. We took the learnings and technology and reapplied them to a different problem in the same market.'

It's also good to know that you are not alone. Even big companies do this, with brands and products. In fact they do it more and more, killing off their newborn babies and in some cases even the talented young adults.

This isn't personal. As the cliches say, most successful entrepreneurs have made mistakes, sometimes tens of times, before they make it big. It is better to learn and come back than to be dragged down by something that isn't going to work.

So what are the key lessons to take out?

It is better to learn and come back than to be dragged down by something that isn't going to work.

1 If it needs a lobotomy and you are not the right surgeon, then don't keep at it. And if no-one you trust can see how it will work, then kill it.

2 Ask someone you trust the straight question – should I give it up? If there is a straight answer then listen. It is often right.

3 If you have spent all the money you said you would and more, then stop now. Do not get into debt. It will have a really negative impact on your reputation if you can't pay the creditors.

4 But think hard about anyone in a different space who might value any of the assets that you have created. They may well and you may be able to extract value from this. If it's technology then ask some techies for help. See if they can work out a way to extract some value by reusing your technology or code. Or see if you can change direction with these assets and monetise it in a different way.

5 People will respect you for taking a tough and objective decision on a very emotional and often irrational subject – your own business. Be happy that you can do that. Many can't.

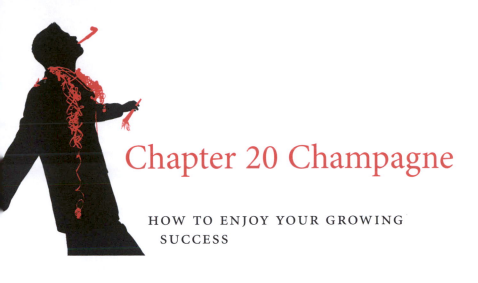

Chapter 20 Champagne

HOW TO ENJOY YOUR GROWING SUCCESS

'How the hell did you spend £900 on a leaving do for Bill when we only made £5000 in sales last month?' John was furious. It was his money and I had taken everybody to a lap dancing club for Bill Zissimopoulous's leaving do in 1996 and things got rather out of hand!

It is all very well celebrating the good times, but not out of proportion with the scale of the business! With hindsight John was absolutely right to be as mad as a snake. My company credit card was swiftly and sensibly emasculated.

Once the revenues begin to come in, then it is easy to get carried away, but it's worth remembering that at this stage you have only just passed stage 1. Just because you are making money doesn't mean you need to blow it rapidly. Still the good news is that it doesn't need to be so hand to mouth. You are out of the danger zone.

Most of the time, of course, you are working like a dog. I was absolutely focused on driving syzygy forward and delivering to clients like Boots, but occasionally you just can't help

There is a temptation to play hard and to excess as you work hard.

letting off steam. There is a temptation to play hard and to excess as you work hard. I can remember holding a client party in 1999 and getting very overexcited. Our most important client, Boots, was there and one of their people was being what I felt was a pain, so I lifted them up and threw them into the buffet of food that we had laid out so smartly! I can't remember who was more surprised – the client himself or the rest of the party – but it was clear that I had overstepped the mark. Not that I showed much remorse. But then we were all on a high and enjoying our growing success, with all the normal trappings of having money to blow on drink and drugs, etc.

Greg Hadfield can remember his son Tom, aged 12, screaming 'We're going to be millionaires' after Greg had persuaded the *Daily Mail* to let him launch Soccernet using the football scores that the *Mail* collected. It was a bit premature, but it's exactly what you might feel when things start to go right!

A key barometer of whether you are starting to be successful is what I call 'the taxiometer'. This is a simple mental test of whether and how often you are prepared to pay to take a taxi to a meeting because it's quicker or will instead take longer and go by public transport to avoid spending the money.

As you begin to start making a success an immediate temptation is to start hiring people to take some of the load but also to accelerate your new-found success. The challenge is to ensure that you only hire the best people. As they say, act in haste and repent at leisure. I hired someone once who I paid more money than I earned and in the end it never worked out. I was desperate to delegate some work to someone else but you can't afford to be too desperate!

And that is the critical part of this journey, setting the right pace for the status of the business. This is true in all ways. One of the ironic and inevitable consequences of burgeoning success is that you get more obsessed with working and building rather than less. In fact strangely the work–life balance goes even more down the drain. You feel re-invigorated and more prepared to go out and sell the benefits of your start-up company. The smart thing though is to work smarter and not harder. It's bloody easy to say this and much tougher to do it, but the real key is to identify what areas of the business have most promise and focus on them. You need to take your early success and ratchet it up further so that your position is better entrenched. Focus on a partner or customer and make something even bigger rather than trying something new. Build from your early successes and in turn this makes you feel more emotionally at ease. Leverage your capabilities now and fast rather than think you have conquered the world.

Use your PR to continue to bolster your every move. When you win an award or a new customer, then leverage that news to create a continuous story of success. People love success

and it breeds more interest and more money.
And apocryphal stories get told and they're great
for publicity!

And sometimes life is a bitch.

You can successfully build a company and then
a recession can wipe out that success. That does
not automatically mean you got it wrong. It may
genuinely be the economy and you don't control
that. But you can take the tough decisions
quickly. If you need to fire people then fire them.
Do it responsibly and indeed do it well, but do
it. Don't bask in past glories at the expense of
common sense. I have been there and took too
long to cut the employee numbers after I floated
syzygy and then didn't cut enough in one and
had to go back for a second cut. It was naive. I
was still basking in my own puffed up self-belief
after a successful IPO. Luckily I have learnt from
that mistake.

And you don't expect to have any issues now.
It's all going right, but as Janie Brown says:
'People don't talk about dealing with quick
success. I paid for a down payment on our
house. It all felt very grown up and satisfying.
But conditions changed. I had 4000–5000
shoes in one factory. They had said that they
had made them, but they turned round one
month before delivery and said they needed
£250,000 up front or they wouldn't deliver.
They hadn't made one pair. Suppliers can be
untrustworthy and buyers can become bullies.
If they decide not to, they don't pay, regardless
of contracts. If you're not a global brand you

can be treated appallingly. What failed is that I never had enough knowledge or tools to manage a business. When Dawn Mello bought my first collection and put it in the best location on her salon floor in Bergdorf Goodman, I didn't realise what she meant when she said, "You're going to need all the help you can get." I didn't know what help meant. I should have consolidated a team and raised money. When I was making money, I should have still raised investment.'

And it's wise to continue to expect the unexpected, even in your personal life. As Ingrid Murray of Ninah Consulting and WeBuyNearby says: 'As a successful woman out socialising, other women assume I would find mumsy talk boring, and men talk to me like a man. So that puts me in no-man's land. Nurturing mother and rational provider, a combination of evolutionary roles.'

Jo Fairley also had to adapt to the unexpected in her personal life as she put it: 'The business started in our house. It eventually took over every room in the house apart from our bedroom. To eat dinner in my house I had to book the room!'

Equally as your success grows then enjoy the good times and make sure that your people enjoy them with you. Relish the moment when you are on CNN or CNBC, even if it is at 6am! But equally take your staff out to the pub. I remember taking all of the syzygy London office of 60 people out for their Christmas party after a highly successful year and sitting back at

> As your success grows then enjoy the good times and make sure that your people enjoy them with you.

dinner and allowing myself a big smile. It was an amazing feeling. I stood up to make a speech to thank everybody for their hard work and someone pushed a Viking helmet on to my head and it did feel like we had conquered the world and that the spoils were there to be had and to be enjoyed.

When I finally got funding for one of the You Wish ventures, I allowed myself the luxury of booking a holiday. Just to dream of being on a beach again, having not had a holiday for 18 months since I started, was amazing. I had taken it for granted that I would have endless holidays as that is what I had always done. When you have really worked at something and it comes good, even if in a completely different way to what you had expected, then you must give yourself some time out and bring back the normal trappings of business life like holidays!

Mark de Wesselow, co-founder of Square Meal, said: 'When you start out, you don't get a high on a Friday evening, but you don't get such a low on a Monday morning either. Now we're more mature, the Friday highs have started to reappear. It's now about what we have achieved that week.'

So what lessons can you apply as you start to get your success?

1 Control your cash. It's bloody obvious as some business things are, but when you have been slaving away in poverty for a while it's very easy to forget this. Make sure you have the cash in the bank before you spend it, especially as a small company.

2 Use PR to create a success story for you. Don't wait for success; pump up your own stories. Create a corporate story for your business.

3 Reward people who have slaved for you. Don't forget them now that you are doing well.

4 Keep focused. Don't overextend either as a business or emotionally. Keep driving the same furrow until you really know that you are secure.

5 Build a buffer. Have spare cash or capacity or a stronger team. Invest in your future. You're only part of the way there.

Chapter 21
Getting out of the ditch

'When it ended, I thought that I was fucked. I
thought that I would never work again because
I had a terrible blot on my career. Everybody could see my
failure and I felt as if I had loser tattooed on my head.'

This is how Seb James described how he felt
after Silverscreen died.

It's horrifying to see how some entrepreneurs
end up in so much trouble, when all they wanted
to do was to work hard and be a success.
When I heard an entrepreneur say 'I
shouldn't be claiming the dole. Not while
I am also earning money doing this. It's
fraud. I could get locked up, but I need
more money to pay the bills. It's going to
take years to get out of this mess.
Christ, what
have I done?'
I shuddered.

The trouble is when your start-up fails and you start to hit the bottom, the only thing you can think of is how to survive, how to protect the people you love. You can be in financial trouble and you will undoubtedly be in emotional trouble. Survival is an incredibly powerful human instinct and it just takes over. It makes you do things that you never thought you were capable of. I have seen people resort to all sorts of crimes to get out of their financial predicaments. It can start as simply as thinking how to avoid paying the taxman something and just escalate from there. After all I don't know anyone who begrudges a bit of tax avoidance, especially if you have no money!

For others it's drink or drugs or extramarital affairs or even a complete retreat from the world and people you know. None of these things are particularly helpful but in their own bizarre way you can believe they're helping you to deal with the stress.

When I left syzygy after six years and having built it up and successfully floated it, I felt massively let down by the shareholders. I felt that they had given time to my other exec board members but had abandoned me because I had a different vision of where the company should go. It took me two years to feel emotionally strong again. Along the way I went round the world on a non-stop party of excess in Rio, Bali, Tokyo, Shanghai, LA, New Orleans and elsewhere. I did everything I could to enjoy life. I went mad. But actually I was miserable. I bitterly resented the fact that I was no longer there, even though I was a significant shareholder myself.

One wrong move can lead to another and every decision piles up more problems. Life is like a decision tree; every step has another consequence and makes it harder to get back to where you started. Once I had left syzygy I didn't want to work again immediately and turned down a couple of fantastic job offers that actually would have helped me recover much more quickly. I was stubborn and angry.

Seb explained to me how he got through it: 'Anyone who embarks on these insane journeys has a low self-worth. I care about implied success. I worried whether I was going to have any friends. Actually no-one cares what you do as long as you are solvent. I got consulting work and I didn't suffer any real financial change, but I was in a very bad way for one year. Like grief I was very depressed. The bleakest days are three days before and two weeks after. The week after we went bust, I went on holiday for a week. When I got back, I was told not to come in. I was bereft as I work all the time and I had none to do.'

So how do you get out of the ditch?

You have to get back to basics – the basics of life. It's like Maslow's hierarchy of needs. You have to take time to rest, sleep and exercise. The things you have neglected for ages. You have to get some work doing something you know how to do. It will make you money. You don't want to try another new thing. You just need some cash

> So how do you get out of the ditch? You have to get back to basics – the basics of life.

coming in and some stability. It's important to get thanked by people for a job well done. It's all part of the process of healing. Only when you start to do these things will you start to build your own self-confidence back again.

It is counterintuitive but actually people and especially other entrepreneurs applaud a fellow entrepreneur who can admit that they didn't make it work and have had to move on. It's honest. It's grown up. It shows experience. It takes guts. It's also very liberating to be able to say I learnt from this and now it's on to something else. The first time it happens it's awful. The second time you have the comfort of knowing that you survived the first time and so you bounce back more quickly.

And sometimes it is a big relief when the pressure ends. Life just rights itself again because you get some balance back in your life.

As Janie Brown said of her business at the end: 'The baby had mutated into a monster. It was a massive needy monster. I had no life. I was flying to China, Italy, the US relentlessly. I realised that doing business in China was madness without my own team established out there. You are going to get slaughtered if you're on your own. It was just at the beginning of the recession. Suddenly everybody wanted money up front. It made sense to pause. From the start of the business to us killing it, the business had changed dramatically. I did not feel it was a personal crisis. It was a huge relief and necessity.

> It's very liberating to be able to say I learnt from this and now it's on to something else.

I used to work in my office and see my au pair playing with my daughter in the garden. I was sickened by it. There was so much passion, so much sacrifice. It was so personal, so intense. I had put so much into it. There is an immediate sense of wastage and loss. But those feelings came and went. I am so grateful that I am in a happier place. Also I have never considered that closing the business is the end of my work. It isn't. I constantly think about starting up again. I am concentrating on my own past mistakes, the flaws in this industry and how to simplify and progress given the changes that naturally evolve in the global market.'

The key lessons for any entrepreneur who hits rock bottom are these:

1 Don't retreat ignominiously. Don't fear the world. Talk to it. Talk to your friends and colleagues. Talking helps you move forward and helps you rationalise it in your own mind. You can't afford to bottle this up any longer.

2 Make a simple plan to move forward. Take some time to rest, have some fun doing something you enjoy and are good at and earn some money.

3 Don't be bitter about what happened. Shit happens. Don't blame anyone or resent the fact that you may have lost some money. Bitterness is so destructive.

4 Don't see what happened as a failure. See it as a learning curve. Get to a position where you can rationally and objectively reflect on what you have learnt from the mistakes. Commit to yourself that you won't repeat them next time.

5 Recognise that you may need more safety nets next time. Maybe you need more financial support. Maybe you need more emotional support. There is nothing wrong in admitting that you can't do everything and take every pressure. There may be contingencies that you can put in place before you start again.

6 Or recognise, as Seb James did, that being an entrepreneur was not the right career: 'It has taught me that I am shit at starting things. It is a rare gift to be able to start things from nothing. That process has eight to ten steps and it's very rare that people can do it. I have actually learnt that I am good at managing big complex problems!'

Chapter 22
Homerun

HOW DO YOU HIT YOUR FIRST
HOMERUN AND LEAVE THE START-
UP PHASE BEHIND?

'I knew I could do well with Feeder. There was no
plan. It was just serious perseverance. I worked very
hard to get my horse in the race.'

Matthew Page said this to me many years after he started to
manage Feeder and had 23 top 40 hits with them.

It reflects the critical point of the start-up
phase. You have to get a homerun. You have to get
in the race. You have to get a score on the board.
When Matthew found Feeder and became their
manager, this was his critical deal in the music
business. The homerun is the first real success
of the start-up. It's the first deal that generates
money. It's the first big success. Basically that
means money and achievement or publicity and
profit. Nothing else matters at this stage.

And you know when you clinch that first
deal or key milestone that you are no longer a
start-up. It's a company-changing experience.

You may retain many of the behaviours of a start-up, but you're probably also trying to behave with more maturity, with a greater sense of belonging. After all, you're making money.

The difference in mood before and after this event is dramatic.

I can remember eSubstance losing money month after month. The mood at the board meetings became gloomier and gloomier as our original investment vanished through the floor. Jeffrey, the CEO, remained relentless in his pursuit of sales and a way out of the impending disaster.

And one day he brought the opportunity to buy a small and profitable contract publishing business, doing the easyJet magazine, to the table. And we did it. The deal transformed the business and we have never looked back. It was all about getting a score on the door. In this case it was in a totally different place to the business that we had started. But that's the key point. Most start-ups end up making money from different products and services than they originally conceived. The challenge is to make money and to get that first homerun.

This isn't just a financial victory. It's an emotional one. You know now you will make it. And success breeds success. At syzygy there was a key moment when we got our first retained client, Mars. It suddenly took us out of the constant scariness of small one-off projects. This was quickly followed by selling a small stake to WPP. That brought obvious financial security with a cash investment into the business, but more importantly it brought us a sense of emotional strength that a small company rarely has. We could stand taller and bigger. And when you have that, you can start to accelerate your growth and leave the start-up phase far behind.

Sometimes the first homerun isn't actually the first big sale or milestone, but the second one, because that then proves that you have a repeatable model. For a while, Icomera struggled to find the right commercial channel for their product. Then they made their first sale to Swedish railway Linx, the first rail company to put wireless Internet access on a train. But actually it was only when they repeated this with GNER in the UK that the company could properly believe that it was out of trouble and even then it still wasn't profitable at this stage. And that can be the problem as a start-up: you may get the first break or hit that first milestone, but it may not be enough. This is especially true with technology companies, who often have to invest a lot of time, money and trials to get their products to break through.

You just need to keep that perseverance going. You need to keep pushing and pushing until enough things are going so right that you know the ditch is long gone.

But you need to keep focus as Nick Wheeler of Charles Tyrwhitt said: 'I nearly go bust when I lose focus. We were a good-quality shirts, ties, shoes and suits company. We thought we could take on the world. We bought six retail shops in

> You need to keep pushing and pushing until enough things are going so right that you know the ditch is long gone.

1994. This lost us more money in three months than we had made in four years. Men just don't buy children's clothes. You just focus and try to be the best in the world at what you do.'

It's also important because in the long run if you don't keep kicking forward you start to narrow your options and in the end this comes back and bites you. Any business always needs to keep moving.

As Matthew Page said: 'In the end I just kicked along with Feeder. I didn't exploit my success. I didn't get out and go go go.'

So how do you do all of this? How do you get that first homerun?

You try out different avenues. You keep experimenting. You try different products. You try different revenue streams. Ultimately if you persevere, you find where your product meets the greatest customer leverage and then you have it. Then you just need to batten down the hatches and make that niche that you have uncovered work. That is when you need to focus like billy-o. You just need to keep going then until you feel that you have broken through.

Jo Fairley reflected: 'An enormous number of people self-sabotage. They choke. They don't make the breakthrough. If an opportunity is there I grab it with both hands.' You have to keep looking for that breakthrough. Until then you're not safe. As Jo continued, 'Ultimately we only knew we were safe when we got the cheque for 75% of our shares.'

In one month You Wish finally got two big

> You find where your product meets the greatest customer leverage and then you have it.

wins. Neither of them were directly to do with the original You Wish idea of being a free concierge for services. The first and most important was that we successfully raised external involvement for a new 'white label price comparison site', using the youwish software as the core of the service. The second is that we launched a new website called Who Gets My Vote? with ITV, prior to the UK general election. This allows UK voters to have an easy way of making an informed choice about who they really want to run the country. You simply select ten policy areas that most matter to you (health, education, tax, etc.) and then a specific policy statement for each one, without knowing which party is promoting it, and then submit your ballot paper to see which party you want! In both cases we did it with business partners and using larger businesses as the route to market. In both cases we leveraged some of the original You Wish assets, whether the software or the thinking in terms of making it easy for consumers to express their needs, but fundamentally we were in a different place.

It's not a homerun but it's on the way. And there are other services in development now off the back of the youwish software and in tandem with business partners!

You also need to keep pushing towards your end goal. You need to take time to get yourself in a position to maximise your final exit. This means thinking ahead all the time. As Hugo Dixon of Breakingviews says: 'We did a good deal with Reuters. Over the years I decided not to solicit interest. I waited for people to come to me. But if I had been more proactive, I could have got an auction going earlier, which would probably have got a better deal.'

The great entrepreneurs often have a level of paranoia about them. This is what keeps them awake and thinking up alternatives. It helps them consider other avenues and ways to exploit what they have started. This is the gift and curse of the successful entrepreneur. As Nick Wheeler says: 'You never know you have survived. It's full of ups and downs. Right now we're booming but three years ago we could have gone bust. Until you can't remember the bad times, you never know!'

Or as Janie Brown admitted, and how many entrepreneurs have been here: 'I never thought I had made it, because I saw no patterns in the numbers to think OK I know where I am. It always felt like a young business.'

William Reeve explained how he could see the solution in the numbers with LOVEFiLM before he got there: 'Once we were at £2 profit per customer per month and we had lower churn rates than the industry then I knew that we could make it. We still needed more customers and I needed further capital to achieve that. But you know you're out of the woods, when you can say we are going to get there.'

As John Bates says: 'Most people think the homerun happens when you reach a high turnover figure, but actually it's only when the business is generating sustainable gross margins and controlled operating costs. As they say: Turnover is vanity. Margin is sanity. Once the business model has been developed and refined and the business is sustainable you *might* get a homerun.'

The key lessons that you need to remember are as follows:

1 Identify your target. At the beginning many start-ups haven't identified it clearly enough. So keep working until you do. You wouldn't succeed as a bomber pilot if you didn't know where to drop the bomb so why expect to do any better with your start-up until you know where you're going?

2 Once you have identified it then put all your efforts into hitting it, into delivering what is required to make it happen. Don't be diverted. It's easy to get sucked into new ideas that might make something better, but don't chase the rainbow, chase what's possible. Be focused.

3 Leverage everyone and everything to make this possible. Take favours off people. Be charming. Use all your powers now. This is when it matters. Don't snatch defeat from the jaws of victory.

4 Make it so emotionally important to you that you can't fail.

5 Look for the second goal as soon as the first one is entering the net. Keep going. Early momentum is everything, if you want to leave start-ups far behind. Soon it'll all be easier!

Summary: Bittersweet

IS IT WORTH IT?

Yes. Nothing would have stopped me the first time, and nothing has stopped me the second and third times, and who knows about the future? The satisfaction you get from taking a company public is beyond words. All the pain and anguish you go through along the way evaporates when you hit a success. And this success is addictive – it drives you to keep going, to find success again and again.

You have a sense of control over your own destiny in a start-up that no other business situation can give you. It's raw. It's natural. It feels centred around your personal goals. It's an amazing feeling.

And entrepreneurial success is much more rewarding than doing it for someone else. It feels better. It feels like a real triumph.

You Wish started out as a consumer proposition – a free concierge for services. But it needed funding to make it happen and I didn't raise that money in 2009, so I stopped it. Nick went to get another job because he needed to earn more money, but he is still actively involved in the next stage of the company's life. Instead I refocused on a business to business proposition using the online platform that we had built, but refocused on providing large companies with innovative ways to cross-sell services to their existing customers. So we have become the You Wish Group. We now conceive, develop and operate innovative digital services for large organisations, using our own proprietary software and as a digital agency.

In March 2010 we successfully raised money for the first of our own price comparison services, which we shall white label to large brands. We have also launched a different service, Who Gets My Vote?, with ITV. It's a website which helps voters to see who they really want to run the country, and we are looking to licence it in other countries. And we now have a number of other services in the making with other business partners, including an online research product. Hopefully these will launch over the next year.

In effect, I have reorganised the business to capitalise on the software that we originally conceived and built, and some of the original thinking, and harnessed them back to a business-to-business model where we get paid for providing services to large companies. We help these large companies cross-sell services to their existing customers. I have also actively sought out business partners who add extra industry knowledge and credibility to our proposition. It seems obvious now, 18 months on, that this is where my strengths lie – selling to large companies. But I was determined to have another go at a consumer business of my own, to try something new and different. Now I am back to what I did at syzygy, but with the insight and learnings of several years running an innovation consultancy.

There were many times when I felt that I might fail. In spite of all my best endeavours, I spent a lot of time being scared and stressed – scared that I might look like a failure and stressed because I had wasted so much money. I also felt pissed off that there is another competitor in the market, making progress with funding, when we didn't achieve it. It really hurts to say that. But, with hindsight, Nick and I did not have all the skills that we needed to make our original idea of a free concierge for services work and did not resolve the channel to market issue that we had from the start because the idea was so ambitious. It has made me difficult to live with. Only my wife, Jo, really saw this and she supported me through it all. It must have been ghastly for her and it's not even over yet. However, I have got a result – not what I expected or what I envisaged at the start. But, nevertheless, a real result. And that is brilliant.

I sacrificed a lot along the way, but 99% of the time you will sacrifice things. Some single-session entrepreneurs can get it right first time around, but it's rare. And every serial entrepreneur that I have met has sacrificed something. This could be missing out on fun times in your twenties, like Mark de Wesselow of Square Meal had to, or missing out on a normal family life, like Peter Christiansen of Precious Media or Roland Rudd of Finsbury Communications had to. It could be money, it could be health, it could be relationships – it could be any of the important things in life.

This is because being an entrepreneur is a life in itself; it's all-consuming. It's full of ups and downs. It's an unpredictable journey and not a straight line, whereas many people's work lives are remarkably stable. They may work hard, they may change jobs or departments, but the fluctuation is minimal and controlled.

And the result you get at the end of the journey is often not what you or others might have expected at the start. Jo Fairley created a rather different family, as she said: 'Green & Black's was a great alternative to a child and one that is going to look after us in old age!' As William Reeve of LOVEFiLM said: 'I am very proud of what I have achieved, of building a £100m turnover business with several £million profits. But I am also sad that I have a sufficiently small shareholding that it was better to leave. After all the hard work it's frustrating that my shareholding got smaller and smaller. I am still the biggest management shareholder but in the end I shall make less money than I did from my first business which had a turnover of £3m.'

And this is why starting a new business is 'bittersweet'; it's a mix of contradictory flavours. And it's constantly surprising – toast and baked beans one day and truffles the next. It's never just a pie!

You learn a lot about business but even more about life.

Many of the business points are so obvious when viewed after time and, indeed, they weren't new to me. I just ignored them. They included some really basic stuff; 'focus', 'customer knowledge', 'channel to market'. I am a better businessman and entrepreneur for having experienced these again, but the real lessons are about me:

- The highs and lows of starting something different can be unbearable. Personally I have finally realised that my tolerance of stress is less than I thought. In truth, I have never been good at being out on a limb and yet I have spent so much of my life doing it. Even aged 21 filming with the mujahideen in Afghanistan, I felt out of my depth and stressed and yet desperate to prove that I was more adventurous than any of my Oxford contemporaries.
- I have realised that much of what I do is driven by a desire to demonstrate my worth, my ingenuity, my ability to conquer new and different things. Ultimately to prove my place in society. The majority of entrepreneurs are driven by the need to prove themselves to their peers. Maybe I don't need to put myself through so much stress again to value myself. Being an entrepreneur can help you see more clearly what you want out of life.
- In future I shall focus ruthlessly on my strengths. Not try to be good at everything. Just be brilliant at what I know I am good at.

- You often have no control over the final balance of success and failure. Sacrifice and success are never delivered in the proportions you expect, so you need to compensate in other ways in your life. You can't just work!

And as Nick Wheeler of Charles Tyrwhitt said, the 'rule of compound growth' is always worth remembering. 'If you start early and keep growing compound growth is massive'. Charles Tyrwhitt now does over £60m of revenues. Perseverance is all. Success is much more likely for those who never countenance failure or have no way out or escape route from the venture that they have started. If you are absolutely emotionally committed then you are more likely to crack it. It's not a 100% guarantee, but it's highly probable.

And now I have my result, my perseverance will kick in again. Onwards and upwards!

And, finally, it really isn't for everyone.

Our society has become obsessed with success, self-improvement and celebrity. It's all about being dissatisfied with who you are and what you are doing and trying to make it better. Everyone is encouraged to start a business, but actually not everyone wants to and not everyone is equipped for it. Many people will prosper and enjoy life more if they don't start a business. But if you want to, and if you do, then you won't regret the journey. You just need to understand what's coming. You just need to be prepared. And then you need to roll with the punches!